MULTI COLLAGEN MAKEOVER

The 28-Day Inside Out Health Transformation

DR. JOSH AXE
AND
JORDAN RUBIN

Notice to Reader

This content is the informed opinion of Dr. Josh Axe and Jordan Rubin, and is for informational and educational purposes only. It is not intended to provide medical advice or to take the place of medical advice or treatment from a personal physician. Readers of this content are advised to consult their doctors or qualified health professionals regarding specific health questions. Neither the author nor publisher of this content takes responsibility for possible health consequences of any person or persons reading or following the information in this educational content. All readers of this content, especially those taking prescription or over-the-counter medications, should consult their physicians before beginning any nutrition, supplement or lifestyle program.

Published in 2018 by Ancient Nutrition

Copyright © Dr. Josh Axe and Jordan Rubin

Visit our website at www.AncientNutrition.com

ISBN-13: 978-0-692-14118-2

Cover photography by Nick Bumgardner and design by Allison Eddy

CONTENTS

HOW TO USE THIS BOOK

This book is designed to educate you on the importance of the most abundant protein in your entire body: collagen. You'll learn how collagen plays a vital role in your health (and appearance), how it functions within the body and why we believe you should have it in your daily diet. Most importantly, *Multi Collagen Makeover* will provide you with strategies and a customized collagen-focused eating plan to help you get your body into a better overall state of health and well-being.

Within these pages, you'll discover all the tools you need to help maximize your body's collagen production. To aid in your success, we've provided The Multi Collagen Makeover Plan (three-day cleanse and 28-day meal plan), a comprehensive shopping list, numerous collagen-boosting recipes and a breakdown of the best collagen supplements you can (and should) take. There's also a Frequently Asked Questions section available online to answer your most pressing collagen-related questions (see Resources on page 152 for more information).

We've even shared testimonials of customers who have tried our collagen-based products, so you'll be able to read about their amazing experiences. Look for these in each chapter throughout *Multi Collagen Makeover*; they'll help to keep you motivated and encouraged as you embark on this exciting new dietary plan.

Are you ready? Let's dive in!

INTRODUCTION

When you think about our modern times, odds are that images of technological advances and social media sites spring to mind. We've become accustomed to a newer, easier way of life. With every swipe of our fingers across our smartphones, we get the instant gratification we're seeking. We live life in the fast lane and barely find the time to slow down, let alone stop and think about where we're headed.

Consider this: Most of us spend our days working hard behind our desks, checking in with loved ones via phone, text or social media sites and sitting in our cars as we're desperately trying to get to our destinations as quickly as possible. And with the increasing presence of fast-food chains and quick grab-and-go dinners on every corner, who has the time to make a home-cooked, nutritious meal when you have an easier, faster option available? If you're like most, you want to be healthy; you want to be fit; you want to lead a well-balanced life in which you feel good about yourself and your decisions. But where do you start? How can we break this vicious, fast-paced cycle with which we've become so familiar?

First, let's take a moment and look at our current state of health. Today, more than ever before, we seem to be surviving and not thriving. We're experiencing lack of energy, intermittent fatigue, loads of stress, occasional discomfort, digestive struggles, brain fog and more. But why is that? In our modern world, with all of our advancements and where health advice is literally at our fingertips 24 hours a day, why do we find ourselves struggling to maintain optimal function?

The simple truth of the matter is that we're so used to our modern lifestyle, it's bleeding over into every aspect of our lives ... including our diets. Compared to the diets consumed by our ancestors, who followed principles of "ancient nutrition" (see page 36 for more information), there are far more nutrient deficiencies in our modern diet. Certain essential nutrients and beneficial compounds that were plentiful in our ancestors' diets centuries or even only decades ago, such as calcium, magnesium, phosphorus, silicon, glucosamine and sulphur, are now largely missing in our everyday meals. And among these nutrients and compounds missing from our diet is one powerful protein: collagen.

THE ROLE OF COLLAGEN

We believe that one major issue with Western, industrialized diets is the decline in the consumption of collagen — the most abundant protein found in the human body. While health experts deem protein as extremely important in the modern diet, many people aren't aware that a high-protein diet in and of itself may not be beneficial if it provides an imbalance of amino acids (the "building blocks" of proteins). Today, most people are consuming only certain amino acids in large amounts, but getting too little of others. For example, real broth and stock, which are excellent sources of important amino acids, have mostly disappeared from our Western diet. Instead, they have been replaced by growing amounts of boneless chicken breasts and other lean meats.

When it comes to striking the right balance of amino acids in the diet, the need to consume collagen-rich foods in place of large amounts of "muscle meat" is often overlooked. Collagen provides a unique blend of amino acids and other compounds, making it absolutely critical for everyone, including: infants, young children, the elderly, athletes, pregnant women, new mothers and adult men and women. Not only does collagen-rich protein share many of the same benefits as other types of proteins, such as helping to support healthy muscles, healthy skin and more, but its benefits extend beyond physical appearance by aiding with everything from gut health to maintaining blood sugar health.

As you'll discover in *Multi Collagen Makeover*, collagen helps maintain the structure and function of almost every part of the body. Our bones, joints, ligaments, tendons, skin and gastrointestinal tract all greatly depend on the consumption of collagen-rich foods, yet top dietary sources of collagen such as bone broth are scarce in today's diet.

We believe that collagen and collagen cofactors (compounds that naturally occur within collagen-containing foods) are the true missing links to modern health. Quite simply, when we don't get enough of the beneficial compounds found in collagen-rich foods, we can experience occasional joint discomfort, hindered mobility, accelerated signs of aging, imbalanced digestion and more. In order to achieve true and lasting health, we must return to following the dietary principles of our ancestors to ensure our bodies get the health-promoting, collagen-rich foods we so desperately need. *Multi Collagen Makeover* will show you exactly how to get the collagen into your diet that is almost certainly missing — the same collagen that was abundantly enjoyed by our ancestors.

DR. JOSH'S STORY

I experienced the powerful benefits of bone broth, one of the richest sources of collagen in the world, for the first time after my mother experienced a health challenge that required nutritional support. Together, my mom and I decided she would follow a nutrient-dense, whole foods diet that would support her gut and immune system health.

Bone broth was one of the key foods my mom consumed almost every day. It provided certain amino acids that were lacking in other protein sources, along with beneficial compounds that improved her energy, sleep and ability to properly digest the foods she consumed. I knew she needed to eat nourishing foods such as chicken broth, berries (rich in antioxidants and vitamin C), wild-caught salmon and veggies (such as leafy greens) daily to start feeling like herself again. She also used nutritional supplements such as beneficial mushrooms, turmeric, vitamin D_3 and frankincense essential oil. I believe this plan ultimately helped support her body's production of healthy cells to defend itself from toxins. It was amazing to see the effects that changing my mom's diet had on her overall health and happiness.

Once I became a chiropractor and worked in private practice, I continued to use real bone broth as part of a nourishing diet with many of my patients. I encouraged my patients to follow a "bone broth cleanse" that could help support healthy joints, ligaments, tendons, skin and digestion. I also recommended that my patients consume a collagen-rich smoothie for breakfast and a collagen-boosting lunch and dinner to support their gut health and promote healthy connective tissue. Just like with my mom, my patients started feeling better after making these dietary changes.

Even after I'd gained experience guiding others in improving their diet and lifestyle, I needed my own digestive support. I was working so hard in my first couple of years in practice — often putting in 70 hours of work each week, plus creating DrAxe.com — that my body really started to become "stressed." I visited an acupuncturist who talked to me about powerful food combinations to support my digestive health. I began making numerous "one-pot" recipes that were used in traditional Chinese health care, such as combinations of herbal infusions and meat/vegetables broths, in hopes of supporting my digestion and overall energy. This was when I started

to consume real bone broth daily and experienced phenomenal results.

I've learned over the years that the benefits of collagen and bone broth go beyond helping support basic bodily functions, by providing foundational nutrition and truly earning the designation as a "superfood." Bone broth and other collagen-rich foods and beverages are important sources of nutrients and beneficial compounds for all of us, no matter our age or current state of health. In fact, my sister is another person in my life who has experienced results from regularly consuming collagen in her diet. She had thin hair and complained about it breaking easily. I recommended that she start consuming bone broth regularly to improve her hair growth, and she was willing to give it a try. After introducing collagen into her diet in the form of Multi Collagen Protein™ and Bone Broth Protein™, she visited her stylist who commented on her thicker hair. My sister also noticed that her nails strengthened and her skin appearance really improved after consuming a collagen-rich diet, which was complete with a collagen-rich supplementation program.

In case you're keeping track, bone broth and collagen as part of an overall healthy diet have helped myself, my mom, my sister and my patients in a variety of ways. Today, I even give our dogs a collagen-rich diet! Their diet includes fish skin, Bone Broth Protein, herbs and berries. This diet has really helped Oakley, our older dog (a Cavalier King Charles Spaniel), with mobility and provides support to his joints. Oakley had severely limited mobility and flexibility. We reluctantly had to keep him in his cage so that he wouldn't further injure himself. But after providing more collagen in his diet by giving him Bone Broth Protein daily, Oakley started feeling much better shortly after (you can check out our dogs on my and my wife's Instagram accounts at @drjoshaxe and @drchelseaaxe).

Today, I try to get collagen into my diet regularly in a few different ways, such as drinking homemade bone broth, cooking with broth and consuming Multi Collagen Protein and Bone Broth Protein daily in multiple recipes, including delicious smoothies. I believe that my collagen-rich diet supports my joints, helps me recover better from exercise, protects the connective tissue in my digestive system and, overall, keeps me feeling good — benefits I can't wait for you to experience as well!

JORDAN'S STORY

I'm of Jewish descent, and I'm sure that just like many Jewish grandmothers, my Polish grandma prided herself on making great chicken soup. In fact, she believed that her prized homemade chicken soup recipe could do just about everything under the sun. That's because Grandma's soup and bone broth were made the old-fashioned way, with organic animal parts that were cooked slowly for many hours, allowing collagen and other valuable nutrients and compounds to be released.

My grandmother and her family definitely practiced a "nose to tail" approach to eating. They consumed bone broth and chicken soup every single week, in addition to eating animal parts that are often looked down upon or discarded today, such as organs, bone marrow, skin and connective tissue. Her family was not the only one benefitting from bone broth — cultures all over the world relied upon traditional stocks and broths made from the bones of chicken, fish and beef to support healthy immune function, healthy bones, healthy joints and much more.

While there were far less studies at the time showing how and why collagen and bone broth were so good for us, Grandma knew that her time-honored soup recipe had health-promoting effects. She was an example of bone broth's benefits, as she remained strong and healthy into older age, exercising daily and carrying pounds of groceries for miles by foot in her late 70s. She taught me about the powerful benefits of bone broth, and this stuck with me when I faced some serious health challenges of my own later in my life.

My grandmother was the first person to introduce me to the many benefits of consuming collagen and its cofactors from real bone broth; the second person to do so was Elaine Gottschall. I came across Elaine's work after struggling with a serious health challenge as a teenager, and her work had a profound impact on me. She was a leading nutritionist who had experience working with people who needed intensive gut support.

Elaine is the author of *Breaking the Vicious Cycle* and the woman responsible for bringing the Specific Carbohydrate Diet (SCD) to the mainstream public. In the 1950s, when her own 4-year-old daughter became very ill with severe ulcerative colitis and chronic intestinal distress that was unresponsive to standard medical therapy, Elaine took matters into her own hands. After seeking out help from

Dr. Sidney B. Haas, who had developed the SCD in the 1920s, Elaine formulated her own dietary plan. Her goal was to honor Dr. Haas's legacy by helping to prevent the needless suffering of people with severe gastrointestinal (GI) issues. Above all, Elaine recommended that people with compromised digestion consume bone broth when they basically couldn't consume any other foods. Just like my grandmother, Elaine stressed the power of consuming real broth and other superfoods and avoiding the consumption of disaccharide-rich carbohydrates such as milk, grains and potatoes.

To help me overcome my health challenges, Elaine recommended preparing homemade chicken soup and consuming it exclusively for five to seven consecutive days. Not only did consuming collagen and bone broth benefit my GI issues, but it also proved to be a very valuable health recommendation for a future challenge I would face.

After I was healthy and fully engaged in my vocation and mission as a natural health practitioner, researcher and author, I recommended the consumption of bone broth to anyone and everyone I could. I shared bone broth recipes in dozens of books I would go on to author, including: *Patient Health Thyself, Restoring Your Digestive Health* and *The Maker's Diet*. Even though I had experienced such great results from recommending and consuming bone broth regularly, I went

through periods when I'd struggle to consume it regularly, mostly due to a lack of time to prepare high-quality broth and difficulty finding good pre-made versions. Then, at the end of 2015, I developed a severe knee issue that immobilized me and landed me on crutches. I found and began consuming copious amounts of frozen organic bone broth once again to help support my joints and tendons (usually 48 ounces of broth per day). Amazed at how well collagen-rich bone broth helped me, I made it the cornerstone of my diet.

Once I began improving, I embarked on a series of health seminars throughout Florida. Fresh off of crutches, I would be required to stand for hours on end. I knew I needed bone broth, so when I asked my mother to make a trip to the local health food store and purchase the foods I needed for my trip, organic frozen bone broth was at the top of the list. Unfortunately, the broth was not available. I realized I was in big trouble without my broth!

Recently, I had begun working on a formulation of a unique collagen supplement for my good friend Dr. Josh Axe. The product would feature multiple types of collagen, including collagen type II, which I sourced from dried, concentrated bone broth. Once I learned that there would be no frozen bone broth waiting for me in Florida, I grabbed a sample of the dried bone

broth to take along on my trip. I mixed one to two tablespoons of the powder with water at least once each day, and it actually tasted very pleasant. Amazingly, I had great results, so I asked my research and development team to run an analysis of the sample and found that, to my surprise, the bone broth powder was nearly 90 percent protein and 60 percent collagen (primarily type II). The dried bone broth contained amino acids such as proline and glycine as well as glycosaminoglycans such as glucosamine, chondroitin and hyaluronic acid; plus, it could be prepared in just minutes (rather than over many hours or even days). At this point, I realized that this was more than a personal health preference: I had found what I believed could be a new breakthrough in nutritional

supplementation! Just like that, the seeds for the creation of Bone Broth Protein were planted.

I'm proud to say that since the time I mixed my first sample of dried bone broth concentrate into water, I've consumed one to three servings of bone broth every day, and one serving in the form of Bone Broth Protein, regardless of where I am and what I'm doing. In my life, bone broth and collagen have proven to be quintessential superfoods. My hope for you is that by reading *Multi Collagen Makeover,* you will be inspired to add this powerful protein to your daily life and share the principles of ancient nutrition with your family, your friends and even your four-legged companions.

CHAPTER 1

A PRIMER ON PROTEIN

If you've ever picked up a weight-loss book or tried a fad diet, you're likely familiar with the word "protein." There's a reason why most weight-loss plans are referred to as "high-protein" diets: Protein is not only the single most important ingredient for building and maintaining your organs, muscles, tissues and cells, it's also present in foods known to boost metabolism and burn fat. Simply put, protein is the body's most vital building block and is involved in almost every function in the body. Without protein, life just wouldn't exist. And since collagen is the most abundant protein in the body, it's important to take a step back and understand what protein is and how it works.

So, what, exactly, is protein? First, it's one of the three macronutrients within the human diet that provide energy in the form of calories (along with carbohydrates and fat). Protein is made up of smaller "building blocks" called amino acids, which are organic compounds chained together in different lengths by chemical bonds. After you eat a source of protein — whether it's meat, fish, eggs or even vegetables such as beans and seeds — the protein is broken down into amino acids. These amino acids then circulate in your blood and contribute to your overall amino acid reserves. Another name for this is the "amino acid pool," which is the entire amount of available free amino acids found inside the human body at any given time.

Protein is used every single day to keep your body thriving and provides the raw materials for your body to remain healthy. Typically, about 16 to 20 percent of the entire body is formed of protein, due to a large proportion of your cells, muscles and connective tissue being made up of amino acids.[1] Throughout each and every day, your body is tapping into its amino acid reserves to carry out numerous functions, including: building connective tissue, helping with hormone and neurotransmitter production, supporting digestion, producing enzymes and antibodies, supporting the immune system and more.

Without enough protein in your diet, damaged tissues cannot be properly repaired, which means your GI tract, skin, muscles and joints can suffer. Likewise, including enough quality protein in your diet will continuously replenish your amino acid reserves and has been shown to help slow the outward appearances associated with normal aging, such as wrinkles, stiffness and immobility due to overuse and loss of muscle mass.[2]

Even if you feel like you eat plenty of protein, you might not be acquiring or maintaining/storing the proper amount of amino acids that you need. Various types of stressors deplete our reserves of amino acids, since they slowly cause damage to cells, tissues and organs. Some factors that can contribute to low amino acid reserves include:[3]

- Consuming a poor diet with mostly processed foods.

- Experiencing high amounts of emotional stress.

- Engaging in either too little or too much exercise without enough recovery.

- Experiencing sleep deprivation.

- Being exposed to environmental pollution (such as from burning fossil-fuels) or the hormones fed to cattle.

- The intensive use of fertilizers and pesticides in agriculture.

- Smoking and excessive alcohol consumption.

- Malabsorption due to digestive issues and other health conditions.

TYPES OF AMINO ACIDS

Before we dive further into how protein benefits the body, let's take a look at the different types of amino acids that form protein. There are two broad types of amino acids: *essential and non-essential.*

Essential amino acids must be obtained from the diet because the body doesn't make these acids on its own, or it makes too little. **Conditionally essential amino acids** are also important to get from your diet, although some can be made by your body. The human body can make 11 of the 20 amino acids that appear within your genetic material, which means that the remaining nine are "essential" parts of your diet.[4]

Essential amino acids include:

- Histidine
- Isoleucine
- Leucine
- Lysine
- Methionine
- Phenylalanine
- Threonine
- Tryptophan
- Valine

Conditionally essential amino acids include:

- Arginine
- Cysteine
- Glutamine
- Glycine
- Proline
- Serine
- Tyrosine

Non-essential amino acids are those that the body can make even without acquiring them from food sources. Therefore, they are typically regarded as less important in the diet. Non-essential amino acids include:

- Alanine
- Asparagine
- Aspartic acid
- Glutamic acid

THE HEALTH BENEFITS OF PROTEIN

Protein is known not only for assisting your body in building muscle, but also for supporting your immune system, hormone production, mental health and even your flexibility. This macronutrient is critical for repairing broken down tissue, replacing worn out cells and producing substances that aid your metabolism, appetite, sleep and mood. Here are some of the many health benefits of consuming protein:

- Supports optimal body composition — one that is leaner and more muscular with less body fat.[5]
- Builds and repairs connective tissue, including muscle, joints, skin and tendons.[6]
- Supports growth and development.
- Facilitates hormone and neurotransmitter production.
- Produces enzymes needed for digestion.
- Supports healthy blood sugar levels (already in the normal range).
- Aids in controlling appetite and reducing cravings.
- Produces antibodies and supports a healthy immune system.
- Supports growth and strength of the skin, hair and nails.

Let's take a closer look at some of these benefits to better understand the role of protein in the body. ▶

Protein and Muscle Building

There are more than 600 different muscles in the human body, which account for about one-third to one-half of your total body weight. Muscles are very "needy" parts of the body, because they require attention on an ongoing basis just to be maintained. If you don't continuously use your muscles and find new ways to keep them challenged, they wind up withering away (a process known as muscle atrophy).

Factors such as age, overall health, activity level, nutrition status and intake of different types of dietary protein all play a role in building and maintaining muscle mass. Generally speaking, the older we get, the less muscle mass we tend to have. The less exercise we do, especially resistance training, the more likely we are to have more body fat and less lean muscle mass.

To be built and maintained, muscles require a combination of activity, nutrition and rest. In order for muscle building to take place, the following sequence occurs:

- Your **muscles are challenged** when they are faced with resistance that requires them to exert force.
- This causes **cellular changes in your muscle fibers**, leading them to become damaged and broken down. (This is why exercise, though beneficial, is considered a form of physical "stress.")
- When muscles are damaged, the nervous system releases inflammatory molecules called **cytokines**. Cytokines alert the immune system that injury has taken place and repair work must be done.
- Given the right nutrition (especially protein) and rest, microscopic damage to muscles are able to be repaired so that the muscles can grow back stronger — a process known as **muscle hypertrophy**.
- The greater the muscular damage, the harder the body works to repair and strengthen it. This cycle of muscles being damaged and repaired builds strength and changes your body composition over time. However, you need the right nutrients in your diet to provide enough energy for this process to take place.

So, how does protein help to build muscle? Dietary protein has been shown to enhance the rate of post-exercise muscle protein synthesis and decrease muscle protein breakdown following resistance exercise.[7]

For decades, it's been known that dietary protein is very important for building and maintaining lean muscle mass — the type of mass that contributes to a strong metabolism, protection against weight gain and increased strength. Following strength/resistance exercise, the body synthesizes proteins for up to 48 hours after training, which is why it's critical to consume adequate protein during this window.

If you exercise and don't consume enough protein afterward, you can actually do damage to your muscles and joints, due to your body entering a catabolic state in which tissue is broken down. In other words, if you don't have enough circulating or reserved amino acids following exercise, you'll wind up being in a negative muscle protein balance that will make it hard to see physical improvements and to reach your fitness goals. The bottom line? You need protein, in the form of amino acids, to work with hormones and growth factors to help repair and build tissue.

Due to its ability to help build and maintain muscle, consuming enough protein is very important as you age. There's evidence that sarcopenia (an age-related decline in muscle mass and a reduction in functional muscular performance) can be postponed or decelerated by engaging in regular physical activity, mainly resistance exercise, in conjunction with eating a protein-rich diet.[8] This combination of diet and resistance exercise during older age has also been shown to be helpful in preventing falls, maintaining strength, improving range of motion and coordination and maintaining everyday functionality.

Finally, protein has additional muscle mass-building benefits, including: supporting hormone balance, boosting circulation and decreasing pain. Collagen peptides (amino acids derived from collagen protein) have been shown in certain studies to positively impact circulation, which is believed to be another beneficial effect in promoting muscle growth, compared with other protein sources.[9] Consuming protein in the form of collagen peptides has also been shown to support healthy joints and functional movement in people dealing with physical limitations.[10] This is a great news, because it may mean that consuming collagen peptides could provide support to people experiencing discomfort while participating in training programs. For more information on how collagen impacts your muscle mass, see 7 Fast Facts on Collagen and Your Muscles.

7 Fast Facts on Collagen and Your Muscles

Here are some facts on collagen and muscle health:

Fact 1: Collagen makes up about 1 to 2 percent of all the muscle tissue in your body, and up to 6 percent of your stronger, larger muscles.

Fact 2: Collagen helps form your muscle tissue because it is a major component of the endomysium, the deepest and smallest component of muscle tissue that covers each individual myocyte (muscle fiber or muscle cells).

Fact 3: Collagen may be especially helpful for building your muscle mass because of the ratio of certain amino acids that it contains. A number of studies have found that muscular strength was significantly improved after a combination of resistance training and collagen peptide intake, compared with the same residence training program and taking a placebo.[11]

Fact 4: Collagen is rich in the amino acids arginine and glycine, both of which are heavily involved in the synthesis of creatine in your body (synthesis means the creation of new proteins from individual building blocks).

Fact 5: Creatine is a substance found in your muscle cells that helps your body to produce energy in the form of adenosine triphosphate (ATP), allowing your muscles to perform heavy lifting or high-intensity exercise. Creatine supplementation has been shown to improve both muscle mass and muscular function in some studies, although not all.

Fact 6: Some research has shown that when more creatine phosphate is created in your body, it leads to increases in total skeletal muscle mass, lean body mass, muscle fiber size, strength and more.[12]

Fact 7: Most studies suggest that consuming protein, including collagen or creatine, immediately after exercise is a better way to facilitate muscle building and improvements in your strength and body composition, compared to consuming it before a workout.[13]

Protein, Connective Tissue and Skin

Connective tissue is a term that describes tissues found in the bones, joints, tendons, ligaments, cartilage, fascia and skin. Its job is to support, connect and/or separate tissues and organs of the body. We can thank connective tissue for basically organizing and holding together the different parts of our bodies.

In addition to holding the body together, connective tissue performs a wide range of functions, such as forming the skin, blood vessels, lining of the digestive tract and parts of the immune system that protect against foreign pathogens. It also gives joints and tendons their mobility, elasticity and strength.

Elastic tissues of the body, including the joints and skin, require a strong and resilient structural framework in order to prevent disease and disability. The framework of elastic tissue is called the extracellular matrix, and collagen protein is a main structural component of the extracellular matrix.

All connective tissue is made of three major classes of biomolecules: structural proteins (collagen and elastin), specialized proteins (fibrillin, fibronectin and laminin) and proteoglycans (units that have a "core protein" attached to glycosaminoglycans).[14] Depending on which class of biomolecules become damaged, various connective tissue diseases can develop. Many skin and connective tissue disorders overlap with each other because they have similar underlying causes. These can include inflammation, autoimmune reactions, allergies, free radical damage and more.

Collagen Protein and Your Skin

Collagen protein is often touted for its skin health benefits. Here's a closer look at how and why collagen protein supports skin health:

 It's your skin's first layer of defense. Protein acts as a support network for the dermis (the skin layer that helps keep skin resilient and supple). The skin is the largest organ in your body and plays a critical role in protecting your insides from the external environment.

 It makes up most of your skin. Roughly 70 to 80 percent of the protein found in skin is collagen. Consuming hydrolyzed collagen has been shown to help increase the density of collagen fibrils and fibroblasts that form the skin.[15]

 It aids skin cell turnover. Because skin has such a tough job, skin cells are constantly being damaged from external factors such as sunlight, abrasions, pollution and more. We need protein, especially collagen protein, for skin cell turnover, or ongoing skin renewal and repair.

In addition to its role in skin health, protein synthesis facilitates the production of other types of connective tissue in some of the following ways:

- Linking collagen fibers together to form a strong matrix.

- Preventing the accelerated breakdown of collagen.

- Facilitating cartilage production and lubrication of joints.

- Helping to differentiate fibroblasts (the cells in connective tissues) from osteoblasts (the cells that make bones).

- Assisting in the normal repair of wounds, abrasions and damage to the skin.

- Forming scar tissue.

- Supporting a healthy digestive tract lining.

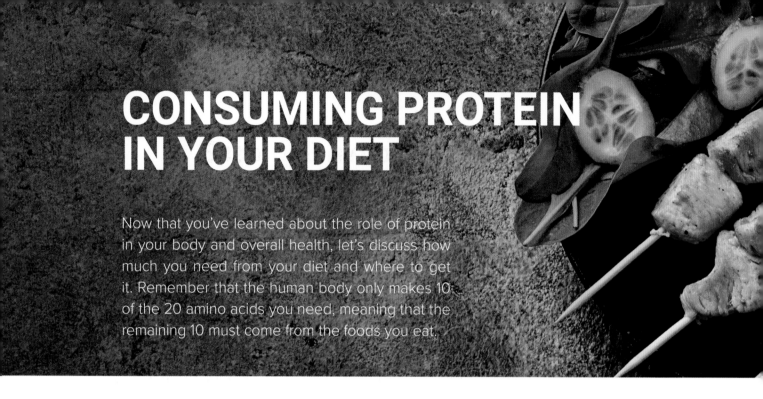

CONSUMING PROTEIN IN YOUR DIET

Now that you've learned about the role of protein in your body and overall health, let's discuss how much you need from your diet and where to get it. Remember that the human body only makes 10 of the 20 amino acids you need, meaning that the remaining 10 must come from the foods you eat.

How Much Protein Do You Need?

The amount of dietary protein you need varies and depends on the following factors: your body size, body composition, physical activity level, gender, age and overall health. A basic recommendation for protein intake is 0.36 grams of protein per pound of body mass for generally healthy adults, or higher amounts up to and beyond 0.64 to 1 gram per pound of body mass in athletes and very active adults.[16]

It's important to note that these recommendations are considered the minimum amounts of protein you should consume daily to prevent protein deficiency and help with protein synthesis. Many experts agree that consuming more protein is ideal for optimal performance, cognitive functioning and overall health.[17] That

said, there is only so much protein your body can store and use at one time, which means there's an upper limit to higher protein intake being beneficial. In other words, unless you are a serious athlete or bodybuilder, consuming more than 0.64 to 0.1 grams of dietary protein per pound of body mass is unlikely to provide additional health benefits.

Keep in mind that since protein is constantly being used by your body, it needs to be replenished frequently. While fat and starch can be stored for later use, the same does not happen with amino acids. It's ideal to consume moderate amounts of protein at regular intervals throughout the day, spreading your protein out rather than consuming very large amounts all at once.

What Are the Best Protein Sources?

Now that you know how much protein you need, let's talk about the best ways to get it. The foods with the highest concentrations of protein are:

Grass-fed beef, lamb, venison and other meats. A three-ounce serving of any of these meats provides about 25 to 29 grams of protein. (Note: While pork is a source of protein, but we don't recommend consuming it due to its tendency to be contaminated with toxins.)

Pasture-raised poultry, such as chicken and turkey. A three-ounce serving provides about 21 to 24 grams of protein.

Wild-caught fish and other seafood. A three-ounce serving provides about 19 to 26 grams of protein. (Note: Shellfish contain protein, but, like pork, they have a tendency to be contaminated, so try to avoid them.)

Pasture-raised eggs. Each egg contains approximately six grams of protein.

Raw, organic dairy products such as milk, yogurt, kefir and cheese. One cup of full-fat yogurt or milk provides about eight to nine grams of protein.

Plant-based foods. To a lesser extent, plant-based foods such as legumes, beans, nuts, seeds, 100-percent whole grains and even some vegetables (such as leafy greens and cruciferous veggies). These range considerably in terms of how much protein they provide, with whole grains, beans, nuts and seeds providing more than vegetables. A ½-cup serving of cooked grains, beans or legumes provides about five to nine grams of protein, while one cup of vegetables provides about two to three grams.

Bone broth, chicken soup and meat stocks and soups. These broths and soups contain soluble proteins, including collagen, that provide powerful support for your connective tissue.

As you'll discover in later chapters, while a high-protein diet certainly has its advantages, one problem with our modern diet is that the vast majority of protein comes from animals that are not grass-fed or pasture-raised. When animals are not raised humanely and in accordance with their natural needs, they tend to become sick and require use of antibiotics, hormones and chemicals, which wind up in the food supply. Typical Western diets also include substantial amounts of "muscle meat," such as lean chicken and turkey breasts but not much organ meat or other animal-based sources of beneficial compounds, such as collagen, that our ancestors frequently consumed. In the next chapter, we'll take a closer look at collagen and its role in whole-body health.

MY BONE BROTH PROTEIN™ EXPERIENCE

❙❙ The Bone Broth Protein powder is not only nutritious, but it has become my secret ingredient in soups and stews! It adds a richness, [along with] protein, amino acids and collagen. I dump a scoopful and let it cook in, then sit back and listen while everyone raves about how rich the soup or stew tastes! It's a win-win! ❙❙

– Lynn B.

CHAPTER 2

COLLAGEN 101

WHAT IS COLLAGEN?

You might recognize the word "collagen" from a familiar beauty product or lotion, or perhaps you've previously heard about the health benefits of consuming it in supplement form. But what, exactly, is collagen, and why is it so important for your body's health and well-being?

Collagen is an extracellular protein (meaning it's located outside your body's cells) made up of amino acids. It accounts for 25 to 30 percent of all the proteins in the human body, making it the single most abundant protein in the body. It is naturally produced in the body and can also be obtained from eating certain foods or taking supplements. Collagen is often referred to as a "complex protein" because it contains a whopping 19 different amino acids, including a mix of both non-essential (made by your body) and essential (obtained from your diet) types. It is the main component within your connective tissue, so think of it as the "glue" that holds your body together.

Just like other proteins in the body, collagen is made up of smaller amino acids. It's formed by linked and winding branches of amino acids (mostly glycine, proline, hydroxyproline and arginine, all of which we'll discuss in detail later in this chapter) that together create longer collagen fibers.

In terms of amino acids, it's important to know that different bodily systems and organs need specific types to serve a variety of functions. In fact, certain amino acids that form collagen have specific benefits for different parts the body; for example, the amino acid glycine has been shown to support restful sleep, healthy blood sugar levels (already in the normal range) and tendon health, while proline is great for skin health.

Where Is Collagen Found in the Body?

Collagen is so important for your overall health that it's found virtually everywhere inside your body — in your muscles, teeth, skin, joints and more. First discovered by researchers in the 1930s, over 28 different subtypes of collagen have been identified to date.[1] The different types of collagen, and different ratios of each type, can be found throughout your body. In fact, collagen helps form many different major parts and processes of your body, including:[2]

- Skin, hair and nails
- Tendons and joints
- Muscles
- Cartilage
- Blood vessels
- Bones
- Teeth
- Intervertebral discs
- Organs
- Scar tissue

When you consume collagen peptides (a peptide is a compound consisting of two or more amino acids) from foods or supplements, they are rapidly absorbed into your small intestine, especially during the "post-exercise recovery window" — when your connective tissues are in need of extra repair. Depending on the location in your body, collagen tissues can be softer or more rigid. For example, the type of collagen found in your bones is more rigid, the type found in your tendons is more flexible and the type found in your cartilage is somewhere in between.

Decoding Collagen Supplements

In supplement form, collagen is positioned and sold in a couple of different ways:

1. **Hydrolyzed Collagen.** This is the type of collagen that has already been partially broken down, making the amino acids easier to absorb (or more "bioavailable"). Creating hydrolyzed collagen involves breaking the molecular bonds between individual collagen strands to release peptides that are digested more rapidly and easily. For this reason, hydrolyzed collagen is typically the type used in supplements, such as protein powders, as it can provide support to people with compromised digestive systems.

2. **Gelatin.** While gelatin is also derived from collagen, it's different from hydrolyzed collagen because it isn't as broken down. In other words, hydrolyzed collagen is gelatin that has been processed more intensively (when gelatin breaks down, it becomes collagen). Gelatin has many of the same benefits as collagen (promoting the health of your joints, GI system, skin and more). You can find gelatin in dried powder form, which is created by isolating and dehydrating animal parts that contain collagen.

How Does Collagen Support Health?

By now, you probably have a pretty clear picture about what collagen is and how it functions in the body: It's one of the major reasons our bodies don't fall apart. Collagen literally functions to help hold you together. Furthermore, collagen synthesis, or the formation of new collagen, is an essential part of normal skin regeneration and also gives structure and strength to your dermal layers.

But collagen's benefits go beyond its ability to promote healthy-looking skin — it's also needed for whole-body health, including supporting joint and tendon health, overall flexibility and strength, better sleep (as it affects neurotrasmitters), digestion and skeletal system strength. Collagen's additional far-reaching benefits include:

- Helping to strengthen cartilage by stimulating chondrocytes (the cells of cartilage).[3]

- Supporting bone mass density.

- Promoting hair and nail health, such as by preventing hair loss and brittle or weak nails.

- Aiding dental health.[4]

- Supporting healthy metabolism and muscle mass.

- Aiding energy output.

- Helping to form the blood vessels and arteries, and supporting healthy blood pressure levels (already in the normal range).

- Aiding the body's use of antioxidants and facilitating the process of constructing healthy cells from DNA and RNA.

- Supporting phase 2 liver detoxification.

- Supporting the central nervous system and promoting relaxation.[5]

MY MULTI COLLAGEN PROTEIN EXPERIENCE

❚❚ I've been adding the Multi Collagen Protein in my coffee every morning, and sometimes in the evenings. I have noticed a difference in my hair, nails and skin. I will never stop using this product. ❚❚

– Nicole C.

How and Why Does Collagen Naturally Deplete with Age?

Unfortunately, your body's production of collagen slows drastically throughout the aging process, and since collagen is necessary for overall physical and mental health, this is a real problem. Keep in mind that collagen is your body's glue, so in your younger years, when there's enough collagen present in your body, you have an easier time "holding yourself together" and maintaining your strength and flexibility. But starting around your mid-30s, you typically begin to produce less collagen, which is why you may start to notice signs of normal aging.

So, why does this happen? Throughout your life, collagen fibers are always being broken down and then regenerated. However, as you age, you have a harder time regenerating collagen at a speed that keeps up with the breakdown rate. Generally speaking, in your 30s, you can expect to lose about 1 to 2 percent of your body's collagen every year, and this rate only increases as you make your way through your 40s, 50s and beyond.

By the time you reach 40 years old, you will likely have lost 10 to 20 percent of your total collagen. Similarly, by the time you pass into your 50s, you will have significantly less collagen available than you did in your teens, 20s or 30s (see Figure 2.1). This decrease in collagen is one of the main reasons that aging is associated with a decline in motor function, muscle mass, flexibility, muscular performance and skin health. To give you a clear picture, there's evidence that collagen production in sun-protected and well-maintained skin of older adults (over the age of 80) is about 75 percent less than the production in the skin of young adults (under the age of 30).[6]

Collagen loss can be accelerated due to unhealthy habits and lifestyles. Additionally, it's been found that collagen loss is associated with high levels of oxidative stress, too much UV light exposure, hormonal imbalances and the use of corticosteroid drugs.[7,8,9] These associations may be related to habits such as eating a poor diet, nutrient deficiencies, smoking and other negative effects that trigger other related health problems, such as joint discomfort or cardiovascular challenges. What does this mean? Basically, it's in your hands: Poor lifestyle choices can hasten your collagen loss, while healthy lifestyle choices can help slow down this process.

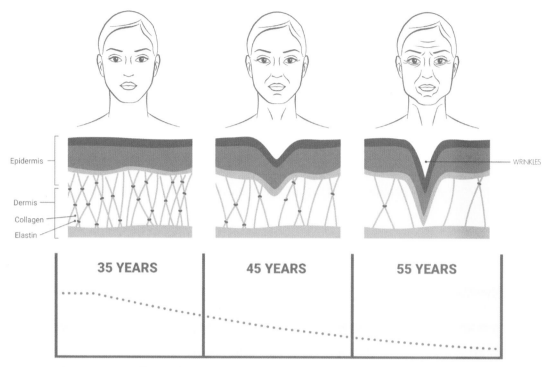

Figure 2.1. Collagen loss with age.

Why Does Our Modern Diet Contain Less Collagen Than Ever Before?

We tend to think of all dietary "protein" as being the same, regardless of the type of food we get it from. But, in reality, this is not the case. To understand why and how we are not consuming the proper "ancestral" ratio of amino acids, let's compare ancient eating examples to today's modern diet.

For thousands of years, animals were eaten "nose to tail," meaning that it was common practice to never discard diverse, valuable parts of a cow, chicken, fish, etc. that were nutrient-dense with vitamins, minerals, antioxidants, and collagen. Instead of discarding those parts, as we commonly do today, our ancestors consumed them in the form of homemade broths and stocks.

Our ancestral cultures actually favored the animals' fatty parts, such as the skin, organ meats, bones and the rich bone marrow. In fact, these parts were prized even more than the animal's lean "muscle meat." Amazingly, these diverse animal parts contain amino acids in different ratios than muscle meat does. They also provide hard-to-get beneficial compounds such as collagen and glutamine. Perhaps our ancestors' wisdom held the key to health all along.

Today, many of us may be experiencing nutritional imbalances in our diets because we consume much more lean muscle meats rather than fatty, gelatinous animal parts that provide higher levels of connective tissue-building amino acids, such as glycine. (Interestingly, studies have shown that consuming glycine can support multiple systems and functions of the body.[10])

Before we dive further into the problems regarding our modern dietary protein sources, let's gain a greater understanding of the different types of amino acids found in animal meat and other parts:

Methionine. Also called L-methionine, methionine is an essential amino acid that has many functions. It is connected to the formation of sulfuric acid and used by the kidneys to acidify urine. Methionine also helps to form bodily proteins and hormones such as L-carnitine, adrenaline, choline and melatonin. While it certainly has benefits, methionine is a precursor to homocysteine, which is an inflammatory protein that in high levels is associated with imbalanced cardiovascular health and fluctuating blood sugar levels.[11] Therefore, consuming too much can be problematic, as it can also alter the body's pH balance (the acid/alkaline ratio), potentially put an undue burden on the kidneys and may promote unhealthy cell growth. People who are low in certain nutrients, including folate, vitamin B_{12} or vitamin B_6, are most likely to experience the negative effects of consuming too much methionine.[12]

BCAAs. Branched-chain amino acids (BCAAs) stimulate protein synthesis and are made of essential amino acids called leucine, isoleucine and valine. Benefits include filling muscle glycogen stores, fueling muscles and minimizing protein breakdown during or after exercise. One example of a common food that provides BCAAs is whey protein, which is why it's often consumed by athletes or bodybuilders. While they're generally safe, consuming too much BCAAs has been linked with increased fatigue and loss of coordination. Additionally, it can be especially problematic for pregnant or breastfeeding women, people with diabetes and those who have difficulty digesting protein.[13] BCAAs are found in muscle meat and other protein sources, but they don't contain certain amino acids found in collagen, such as proline and glycine.

Proline. Proline and glycine are the primary types of amino acids found in collagen chains. It makes up about 15 percent of collagen, and together with glycine and hydroxyproline, proline represents around 50 percent of the total amino acid content of collagen. It is considered a non-essential amino acid, because the human body can synthesize some on its own. Its roles include helping to regenerate cartilage, form connective tissue, promote skin health and support joint health. Proline also helps with functions of the cardiovascular system, especially of the arterial walls, such as preventing fat from accumulating in the bloodstream. Some of the major benefits of proline include: promoting the health of skin, supporting immune system health and antioxidant status, aiding the metabolism and synthesis of other compounds, acting as a signaling molecule and a sensor of cellular energy status, supporting healthy blood pressure levels (already in the normal range), and aiding fetal growth and development. Proline is converted into hydroxylysine and hydroxyproline in order to help form collagen. Supplementing with proline has been shown to support the production of collagen and, therefore, may help reduce signs of normal aging due to declining collagen, such as wrinkles and loose or sagging skin.

Glycine. This amino acid is important for supporting gut health, restful sleep, healthy blood sugar levels (already in the normal range) and tendon and joint health. Glycine makes up approximately 20 to 30 percent of the protein found in collagen. It's the smallest amino acid and one of three amino acids that form creatine, which promotes healthy muscle growth and boosts energy production. Glycine is also one of three amino acids shown to stimulate the body's production of glutathione, known as the master antioxidant. While collagen sources such as bone broth provide a good dose of both glycine and proline, muscle meat does not.

Hydroxyproline. A major component of collagen, hydroxyproline comprises about 14 percent of collagen. It helps to make collagen stable and is particularly abundant in gelatin after collagen is broken down. Like proline and glycine, hydroxyproline is considered a non-essential amino acid, but acquiring more of this amino acid from your diet has additional benefits for your joints, skin and other tissues.

So, what's the state of the protein comprising our modern diet?

First, muscle meat — such as hamburgers, ground meat, chicken breast or turkey — is the most abundant source of protein in the modern Western diet.[14] These foods are high in certain types of branched-chain amino acids that are deemed essential. They provide all amino acids, which is why they are called "complete proteins," but have a higher proportion of tryptophan and methionine compared to other amino acids. Many of us consume large amounts of these branched-chain amino acids because we regularly eat protein sources like lean meats, fish, dairy and eggs; in fact, many people wind up consuming very high amounts of protein — often more than they really need! Consuming too much protein has actually been shown to tax the kidneys and liver and can wind up contributing to health challenges, such as digestive issues.[15]

While lean meats are very low in glycine, this beneficial amino acid is found in high amounts in food sources of collagen. Bone broth, organ meats and connective tissue from animals (all sources we don't typically consume in our modern diet) are high in glycine but low in methionine. In contrast to muscle meat, collagen contains virtually no tryptophan and very low amounts of isoleucine, threonine and methionine. Consuming bone broth and other sources of collagen has been shown to help balance amino acid intake, such as increasing glycine and lowering methionine. This may support already-healthy blood pressure and metabolic levels, a healthy inflammation response and better focus.[16,17]

For some time, collagen was generally regarded as having a "relatively low biological value," mainly due to the low amount of branched-chain amino acids (BCAAs) and lysine it provided. In recent years, however, beliefs about collagen's effects versus other protein sources have shifted. For example, in one study, when compared with whey protein, the amino acids found in collagen were shown to better support both nitrogen balance (important for exercise recovery and muscle growth) and healthy body weight during a low-protein diet.[18] In short, collagen helped improve the availability of essential amino acids.

Remember that when it comes to maintaining your health, the goal is not to consume very high amounts of protein from any and all sources. Instead, you should focus on getting the amount that you actually need and striking a balance in your diet of the different, beneficial amino acids.

MY BONE BROTH COLLAGEN™ EXPERIENCE

❚❚ I absolutely love my Bone Broth Collagen Vanilla powder and take it religiously twice a day in my coffee or shake. I noticed an improvement almost immediately, and my skin looks amazing. I have tried other products ... and this one is the best. It's the closest thing to making my own bone broth that I have found; I am a customer for life! ❚❚

– Aimee M.

CHAPTER 3

ALL ABOUT COLLAGEN: TYPES AND COFACTORS

COMMON TYPES OF COLLAGEN

To truly understand how collagen works in your body, you must first learn about the different types of collagen. As we discussed in Chapter 2, researchers have identified at least 28 different types of collagen, and at least 16 types are found inside the human body. These include collagen types I, II, III, V and X.[1]

So, what makes these collagen types different from one another? It really comes down to the variation in the sequence of amino acids found in each type. The different types of collagen vary in their exact molecular isoform structure and their polypeptide chains. These differences are determined by DNA, which hold the body's instructions for making all types of collagen.

The vast majority of collagen found throughout your body are types I, II and III. Together, these three types account for about 90 percent or more of all collagen in your body. Types I, II, III, IV, V and X account for about 99 percent of all the collagen in your body.

While collagen type I is by far the most abundant in your body, you still need the other types of collagen as well, due to their special properties. While they have their differences, all collagen types have one major common responsibility: They act like the body's natural "glue." Remember, collagen helps to hold the body together, supports cohesion of different organs and systems and helps give the body's structure its integrity, resistance and flexibility. This is true for all the different types.

Here's an overview of the different types of collagen, including the best sources and primary benefits of each:

Type I: Considered to be the strongest type of collagen found in the human body, type I is found throughout your body in many different locations — primarily in the tendons, joints, ligaments, bones and skin. It can also be found in your organs, scar tissue, teeth and arteries. Collagen type I is made of mostly eosinophilic fibers that help hold together your body's structure.

Studies have found that collagen type I is very important for skin health, including aiding normal wound healing and helping to form scar tissue. It helps to give skin its stretchy and elastic quality and aids in supporting skin health and normal regeneration. Type I collagen fibrils have a great deal of strength and can be stretched without being broken. In clinical settings, a soluble form of type I collagen is used as an adhesive substrate for cell cultures and for regenerative applications. These include using it in cosmetic surgery, dermal injections, bone grafting and reconstructive surgery.[2]

Some of the best sources of type I collagen include: bone broth, grass-fed bovine/beef collagen (cartilage, bones and hides of cows), eggshell membrane collagen and fish collagen (sourced from the scales, skin, bones and fins).

Type II: Thought of as the body's "sponge" material, type II collagen aids your flexibility and range of motion. Its most important job is to help build cartilage, which is found in connective tissues, including the joints that cushion the spaces between bones.[3]

Both animal and human studies suggest that cartilage made in part by type II collagen can help support joint health, which is especially important in older age, when occasional discomfort is often more common. Type II collagen is also important for supporting joint health and discomfort due to overuse.[4] A randomized, controlled study evaluated the oral use of type II collagen on markers of cartilage degradation in individuals and found that collagen supplementation helped improve walking ability, mobility and flexibility.[5]

One of the best sources of type II collagen is poultry broth (from chicken, duck or turkey sources).[6]

Type III: This collagen is made of reticular fibers and is a major component of the extracellular matrix that makes up organs and skin. It mostly helps to form meshy, delicate tissues that encase your vital organs, especially your liver, lungs and arteries. It's also found in your bone marrow and lymph nodes.

Type III collagen is important for the development of the cardiovascular system and for maintaining normal physiological functions of the heart and arteries throughout adult life. Because type III collagen provides support to blood vessels and tissues of the heart, depleted levels have been linked to blood vessel instability.[7]

One of the best sources of type III collagen is bovine collagen, and, in lesser amounts, eggshell membrane collagen.[8]

Type IV: Type IV collagen primarily helps to form tissues of your internal organs, including the tissues within your respiratory tract, such as the lungs and bronchial tissue. It also forms parts of your kidneys, heart and digestive system, including the tissues surrounding your intestines.

Type IV collagen has the important job of forming basal lamina, which is found in endothelial cells that surround and cushion organs, muscles and fat. Basal lamina fill the spaces between the top layer of skin or tissue and the deepest layer. They have a gel-like fluid that provides padding and absorbs shock. Basal lamina are also needed for nerve and blood vessel functions, and they help to support healthy immune system function.[9]

Studies have found that people with high blood sugar levels tend to have lower levels of type IV collagen, as they excrete more of this collagen through their urine, which may be linked with kidney challenges.

The best source of type IV collagen is eggshell membrane collagen.[10]

Type V: This type of collagen helps to form your hair, the placenta in pregnant women and also the surfaces of cells. There are an estimated 70 trillion cells in the human body, and each has a surface that is made in part by type V collagen.

Type V collagen is needed during pregnancy because it helps to form a healthy, strong placenta — the organ that develops in the uterus, provides oxygen and nutrients to the growing baby and removes waste. A study that examined 14 normal human term placental tissue samples found that type 5 collagen was strongly immuno-supportive and important for forming areas of the stem villi stroma in the placenta (these provide maximum contact between the fetus and maternal blood).[11]

Some of the best sources of type V collagen are bovine collagen and eggshell membrane collagen.[12,13]

Type X: Finally, type X collagen mainly aids in the formation of both new bones and articular cartilage (the smooth, white tissue that covers the ends of bones where they come together to form joints). As a result, this collagen is beneficial for supporting overall bone health as well as the synovial joints (joints that connect bones with a fibrous joint capsule that contains lubricating synovial fluids).

A 2005 review found evidence from multiple studies that type X collagen plays a role in the growth, development and remodeling of articular cartilage. It supports the process of endochondral ossification, which is how bone tissue is created in mammals through the use of minerals and collagen. Type 10 collagen facilitates endochondral ossification by regulating matrix mineralization and matrix components, which takes place before new bone formation.[14]

The best sources of type X collagen are chicken collagen and eggshell membrane collagen.[15]

Notable Types of Collagen

Collagen Type	Location in the Body	Major Functions	Best Sources
Type I	Tendons, joints, ligaments, bones, skin, organs, scar tissue, teeth and arteries	Promotes skin elasticity and overall skin health	Bone broth, bovine collagen, eggshell membrane collagen, fish collagen
Type II	Connective tissues, such as joints	Builds cartilage; aids flexibility and range of motion	Chicken collagen
Type III	Tissues surrounding the liver, lungs and arteries; in bone marrow and lymph nodes	Major component of the extracellular matrix that makes up organs and skin; promotes skin	Bovine collagen, eggshell membrane collagen
Type IV	Tissues within the respiratory tract, kidneys, heart and digestive system	Helps form internal organ tissues; forms basal lamina	Eggshell membrane collagen
Type V	Hair, placenta (in pregnant women) and on the surface of cells	Helps to form hair, the placenta in pregnant women and cell surfaces	Bovine collagen, eggshell membrane collagen
Type X	Articular cartilage	Aids both new bone and articular cartilage formation; supports bone strength and synovial joints	Chicken collagen, eggshell membrane collagen

THE IMPORTANCE OF COLLAGEN COFACTORS

Now that you have a better understanding of the most prevalent types of collagen in your body, let's discuss the compounds that support the production and function of collagen within your body. These compounds are often found in collagen-containing foods or supplement form and are known as **collagen cofactors**.

What Are the Main Collagen Cofactors?

Each cofactor has its own unique benefits and works with collagen. The main beneficial collagen cofactors include:

Glucosamine. Glucosamine sulfate is a compound naturally found within the cartilage of your joints that helps with lubrication and absorbing shock. It can also be obtained from consuming poultry (chicken) bone broth. Glucosamine is an aminosaccharide that helps create cartilage from compounds called aggrecan and proteoglycans. This cofactor supports healthy joint function and has healthy aging properties, giving it the ability to help with occasional discomfort.[17] In fact, if the name sounds familiar, it's probably because glucosamine is one of the most common supplements taken by people seeking to promote flexibility and mobility.

In addition to supporting joint and ligament health, glucosamine has many other benefits such as: supporting gut health, aiding mobility and range of motion in athletic or active people and supporting healthy bowel function.

Chondroitin. Chondroitin is found in the human body primarily in cartilage. In supplement form, it's derived from the natural cartilage of animals such as chickens. It's found in high amounts in their bones, skin and tissues and can be obtained from drinking chicken bone broth.

Like glucosamine, chondroitin is commonly taken by people to reduce occasional discomfort and discomfort due to aging or injury.[18] Chondroitin may help to support a healthy inflammation response and is commonly considered to be safe. In addition to promoting joint health, chondroitin is beneficial for the following: helping the body synthesize new cartilage, aiding in keeping the body flexible following exercise and supporting normal wound healing.

Hyaluronic acid. Hyaluronic acid is a lubricating, clear substance that's naturally produced by the body and found in the greatest concentrations in the skin, joints, eye sockets and in other tissues made of collagen. It's known to support the skin's texture and appearance and to support joint health.[19]

This cofactor is commonly used in healthy-aging serums, joint-supporting formulas, eye drops and lip balms, due to its ability to help prevent water loss. Daily topical application of serums containing around 0.1 percent of hyaluronic acid can help support skin hydration, may minimize wrinkle appearance and aid in boosting skin elasticity. Eye drops containing this cofactor may help to keep eyes moisturized and prevent light damage.

Why Are Collagen Cofactors Important?

Your body needs collagen cofactors for the synthesis of certain proteins and lipids (fats) that form important tissues, especially cartilage. For example, glucosamine works with collagen to form connective tissue that make up parts of the digestive tract and immune system. Collagen cofactors can also help to retain collagen, making it more effective. For example, hyaluronic acid helps to boost collagen in the skin and joints and, therefore, supports skin moisture, elasticity and flexibility. Cofactors are also beneficial for supporting healthy inflammation response and reducing free radical damage.

As you can tell, collagen cofactors are responsible for numerous critical roles within the body. Some of these roles and responsibilities include:[15,16,17]

- Helping to reduce oxidative stress that can diminish collagen.
- Supporting joint health, mobility and flexibility.[20]
- Forming cartilage that surrounds the joints.
- Helping to reduce occasional aches, pain and muscle soreness due to strenuous exercise and overuse.[21]
- Forming synovial fluid that provides lubrication to the joints.

- Supporting exercise recovery.

- Aiding in building tissues of the gastrointestinal tract.

- Supporting healthy immune system function and gut health.[22]

- Supporting bone health.

How Much of These Cofactors Do You Need?

While there is currently no standard recommended daily allowance (RDA) or intake of collagen cofactors, studies suggest that most adults can benefit from taking certain amounts per day, often combined with one another. To support collagen synthesis in your body, here are some guidelines below:

Glucosamine: Aim to consume 500 to 1,500 milligrams of glucosamine sulfate daily.

Chondroitin: Take 800 to 1,200 milligrams of chondroitin sulfate daily, in three divided doses.

Hyaluronic Acid: When taking hyaluronic acid, aim to consume about 50 to 80 milligrams orally once or twice each day. Hyaluronic acid can also be found in many topical applications, such as creams and lotions. If you're interested in using it in topical form, look for a product with a concentration of about 0.1 percent.

MY BONE BROTH PROTEIN EXPERIENCE

❚❚ I was in need of joint support in my feet, after hearing and reading good things about turmeric and bone broth, decided to try the Bone Broth Protein Turmeric. After a month on the powder, I have increased flexibility and mobility, and I am definitely feeling way better overall. ❚❚

– Jaime L.

CHAPTER 4

HOW TO CONSUME MORE COLLAGEN

Not only does your body make its own collagen, but by now it's probably clear that you can also get collagen from eating certain foods and taking collagen supplements. So, where do you start? What are the best ways to get more collagen in your diet?

Here are the top three things to do in your quest to consume more collagen:

1 Incorporate all-natural, collagen-promoting foods into your diet.

2 Consume collagen supplements.

3 Eat a well-rounded diet that aids the absorption of the collagen you consume.

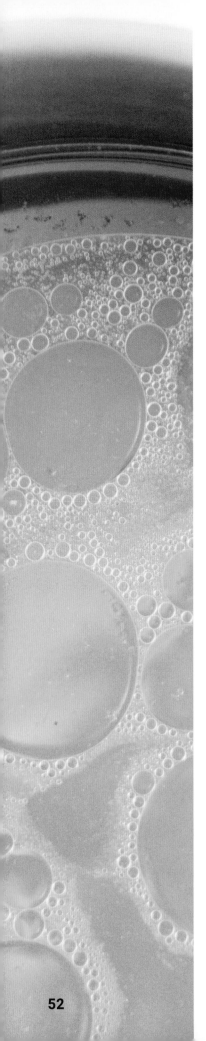

THE BEST DIETARY SOURCES OF COLLAGEN

While you'll find a comprehensive listing of *Multi Collagen Makeover* foods in Chapter 6, the following pages contain an overview of the top collagen-containing foods you should be consuming regularly, including: bone broth, poultry, red meat, fish and eggshell membrane. Read on to discover why these foods are excellent sources of collagen and how they're best consumed.

Bone Broth

Hands down, our favorite source of collagen is bone broth — a traditional food that has been consumed for thousands of years by people living all around the world. When it comes to getting more collagen in your diet, the first step we recommend is making and drinking/consuming real bone broth, whether it's homemade or store-bought.

Bone broth is commonly considered a "superfood" because it contains amino acids such as glycine, proline and arginine, in addition to glucosamine, trace minerals like calcium and phosphorus and a number of other beneficial compounds.

Bone broth can be consumed on its own (you can drink it plain or use it in recipes like soups or stews). Alternatively, if you prefer to save time, you can use Bone Broth Protein

or Bone Broth Collagen (see pages 58 and 60-61 for more information on these products) in all sorts of sweet and savory recipes, depending on the type of product you use. Additionally, you'll find a detailed meal plan in Chapter 6 that includes many recipe ideas containing multiple bone broth-based products. Examples include: protein smoothies (you can mix collagen powder with your other favorite protein powders), pancakes, soups and more.

Poultry

Chicken collagen is the best source of type II collagen and a very popular collagen used in supplements.[1] (You'll recall from Chapter 3 that type II collagen supports the health of your joints, digestive system and immune system.) This type of collagen is found in the cartilage, bones and other tissues of chickens (such as chicken feet, which is a traditional food eaten in many parts of the world). Other poultry sources of collagen include the connective tissue of free-range turkeys and ducks.

Chicken collagen contains amino acids such as glycine, glutamine and proline, plus chondroitin and glucosamine (two compounds that help support normal cartilage rebuilding). One study found that supplementing with type II collagen helped support joint function in adults when compared to placebo, and it was well-tolerated.[2] Researchers hypothesized that type II collagen helps to promote joint health because it induces the migration of T-regulatory cells to the area of greatest need.

You can consume chicken collagen by eating chicken cooked on the bone with its skin, or by making chicken broth, soup, stew and other savory recipes with a variety of animal parts (such as organs, bones, etc.).

Red Meat

When you eat animals "nose to tail," you're consuming collagen from all parts of the animal, including the bones, connective tissue and muscle tissue. Bovine collagen is a naturally occurring protein found in the skin, bones and muscles of cows and cattle.

This type of collagen provides both type I and type III collagen. These two types of collagen work together in many ways to help support the health of your skeletal system, cartilage, bone marrow, skin and joints.

Collagen types I and III are the major components of skin, hair, nails, muscles, tendons, ligaments, bones, gums, teeth, eyes and blood vessels. Because bovine collagen is a great source of type I collagen, it's commonly considered a versatile superfood that supports many types of connective tissues in the body. Additionally, it has been shown to help with the proliferation and differentiation of the cells that form bone tissue, making bovine collagen an ideal source for supporting bone health.[3]

Bovine collagen is rich in the amino acid glycine, which supports creatine synthesis and helps to build muscle mass. It also provides proline, which supports skin health (the reason that some use it to help promote healthy skin).

To get more bovine collagen into your diet, consume beef broth, soup, stew and other savory recipes with a variety of animal parts (organs, bones, etc.). You can also consume hydrolyzed collagen protein powder (sometimes called collagen hydrolysate), or gelatin (a form of that absorbs liquid and forms a gel in recipes). Look for high-quality, grass-fed bovine collagen supplements. Collagen protein powder made from bovine collagen can be used just like other protein powders, such as in smoothies or baked goods. (Having a collagen smoothie after a workout may help to support normal muscle growth and recovery.)

Aside from consuming bovine collagen, you can also use it on your skin; applying a cream with 5 percent bovine collagen two or more times daily may help offer skin support.

Fish

Fish collagen (sometimes called marine collagen) is one of the most sustainable and absorbable sources of type I collagen. Fish collagen is sourced from the parts of fish, including their bones, scales and fins. Its increased absorption rate and bioavailability are due to the smaller particle size of fish collagen peptides. Collagen from fish has been shown to support accelerated matrix mineralization and to have a positive effect on osteoblastic cells that help to build bone mass.[4]

You can get fish collagen in your diet by eating pieces of fish that contain small bones (such as canned salmon or sardines), tissues or scales, or by making fish stock/broth, soup and stew with a variety of fish parts (such as with fish heads).

Eggshell Membrane

Eggshell membranes provide types I, V and X collagen. Found in each of the two layers of the eggshell membrane, collagen provided by eggshell membranes may support skin health, normal wound healing, hair growth, cell surfaces and the placenta in pregnant women.[5]

The type V collagen provided by eggshell membranes is made of fibrillar collagen molecules that are composed of one or more types of alpha chains. It supports the functions of other collagen types, including types 1 and 3, and contributes to the bone matrix, formation of the cornea and the interstitial matrix of muscles, liver, lungs and the placenta.[6]

Eggshell membrane has been shown in certain human studies to help prevent the accelerated aging of skin and reduce damage caused by UV-light. Research suggests that eggshell membrane helps to form the superior protective layer of moisture in the skin and also helps support normal microbial balance.[7]

Since most people don't typically eat eggshells, consuming supplements such as a multi collagen protein powder made with dried eggshell membrane collagen is usually the best way to consume this beneficial ingredient.

TOP COLLAGEN SUPPLEMENTS

Can you get enough collagen from supplements? Simply put, it's best to consume collagen from both natural food sources and supplements (just as with other nutrients, vitamins and minerals). Collagen supplements can really come in handy because they save you loads of time and effort; for example, Bone Broth Protein takes the work out of making slow-cooked bone broth over the course of a couple of days. Here are some of our recommended collagen-based supplements.

Multi Collagen Protein

In supplement form, especially as protein powder, collagen is easy to use. It's virtually tasteless and odorless, plus soluble in hot or cold liquids, including coffee, smoothies and baked goods. It's beneficial to consume just about any time of day but especially before and/or after workouts.

So, what makes Multi Collagen Protein powder different? First, it contains more than one type of collagen, and it's sourced from four food sources. Multi Collagen Protein Powder features collagen types I, II, III, V and X. Second, it is derived from a combination of beef, chicken, fish and eggshell membrane collagens, giving you a wide range of collagen types.

Containing 7 to 10 grams of protein per serving, Multi Collagen Protein powder features hydrolyzed collagen peptides that are easy to digest. It's also made without milk, shellfish, tree nuts, wheat, peanuts or soy, making it suitable for those with many types of sensitives.

Multi Collagen Protein mixes instantly into liquids and can be incorporated into recipes as well. We recommend using one serving (one scoop) as desired. Use this collagen powder just as you would other protein powders. Try mixing a scoop into 8 ounces of water or another liquid (such as coffee, tea, juice or almond milk) and shake, blend or stir to help dissolve the collagen. You can also add this supplement to baked recipes such as muffins, bars or pancakes to increase the protein content.

NEW
MULTI COLLAGEN
OFFERINGS

Bone Broth Collagen

Thanks to recent advances in bone broth processing techniques, you can now consume bone broth much more easily by using dried, powdered Bone Broth Collagen. This product is groundbreaking because it's derived from real, whole-food bone broth, yet it's shelf-stable and ready to consume in less than a minute. You can either take Bone Broth Collagen capsules or Bone Broth Collagen powder mixed with your favorite beverage or incorporated in many delicious recipes. The powder easily and instantly dissolves in water, providing you with all the benefits of homemade bone broth in just seconds.

Each serving has approximately 10 grams of easily-digestible collagen. It provides types I, II and III collagen from real food sources, including chicken, beef and turkey. Bone Broth Collagen is also Paleo friendly, gluten free and made without dairy, soy, grain or nuts. It can be mixed into liquid or incorporated into smoothies and other recipes.

Organic Bone Broth Collagen

Each serving of this Certified USDA Organic product features easily-digestible collagen. It provides type II collagen and is sourced from organic chickens. Just like real bone broth, it provides chondroitin sulfate, glucosamine sulfate, hyaluronic acid and trace minerals.

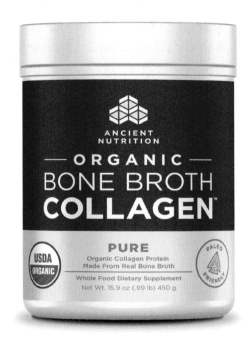

Organic Bone Broth Collagen comes in a variety of flavors, including "pure" (flavorless), vanilla and chocolate. Pure makes a great addition to drinks, marinades and savory dishes, while the vanilla and chocolate flavors can be used in baked recipes, smoothies and more to add protein plus a bit of sweetness.

KetoCOLLAGEN™

As we've discussed, collagen provides a unique blend of amino acids and other beneficial compounds associated with healthy joint function, making it absolutely critical for everyone. This is especially true for those following a ketogenic diet: a high-fat, moderate-protein, low-carb dietary plan that "tricks" the body into thinking it's fasting through strict elimination of the amount of glucose consumed. When glucose is severely restricted in the diet, the body enters into a health-promoting state of ketosis — a metabolic state that occurs when a portion (small or large) of the body's energy comes from ketones in the blood, rather than from glucose. In short, it positions the body to burn fat as fuel.

Containing 15 grams of protein per serving, KetoCOLLAGEN is powered by bone broth and features a special blend of hydrolyzed bovine hide collagen peptides and medium-chain triglycerides (MCTs) from coconuts. It's free of gluten, dairy and soy, making it a suitable collagen supplement for keto dieters with food sensitivities.

KetoCOLLAGEN mixes well into water, almond milk, coffee or tea and can be enjoyed in both warm and cold beverages. It can be incorporated into your favorite recipes as well, including smoothies and baked goods.

MY KETOCOLLAGEN EXPERIENCE

❚❚ Since I just started keto, I was thrilled to find KetoCOLLAGEN from Dr. Axe. It is all grass-fed, pasture-raised beef. [You] can't find that much anymore. I was on his other collagen for a year with fabulous results in my nails, hair and skin. I am continuing to see great results with this one, especially in my nails — no more ridges! Will definitely reorder. **❚❚**

– Ann M.

Bone Broth Protein

While Bone Broth Protein is similar to Bone Broth Collagen, it has a slightly different texture and typically is consumed in higher amounts to increase protein intake, making it helpful for supporting normal muscle synthesis. Compared to collagen powder, Bone Broth Protein powder is thicker and a great addition to recipes to make them more filling. It provides mostly type II collagen, while Multi Collagen Protein provides types I, II, III, V and X.

Just like real bone broth, Bone Broth Protein contains 19 different amino acids, such as glycine, proline and hydroxyproline. It also provides minerals, including calcium, magnesium and potassium and is a good source of glucosamine, chondroitin and hyaluronic acid. Bone Broth Protein is sourced from poultry, which is why it's rich in type II collagen.

Bone Broth Protein can be taken in capsule form or used as protein powder in all types of beverages (such as water, coffee, juice, tea and almond milk) and recipes. It has between 0 to 2 grams of sugar (added or natural), has between 0 to 2 grams of carbs and supplies 20 grams of real, whole-food protein per serving (about 20 grams). It's Paleo-friendly and safe for people with sensitivities to dairy, grains, gluten, peas, soy and nuts.

A simple way to instantly make bone broth is to mix one scoop of Bone Broth Protein with 12 ounces of water. Additional ways to use Bone Broth Protein include adding a serving to a shake or smoothie before or after a workout, consuming it as a filling snack between meals, using it to make a fast but nutritious breakfast or adding some right into your favorite baked goods.

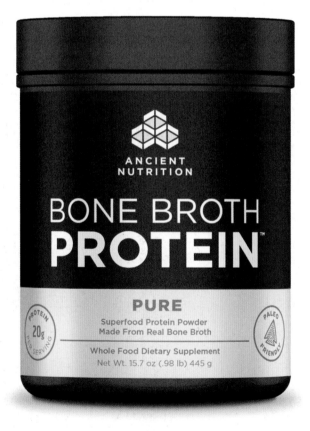

Organic Bone Broth Protein

Organic Bone Broth Protein offers all the same convenience and benefits as Bone Broth Protein, plus it's sourced from organic chickens. It's Certified USDA Organic, gluten free, contains no preservatives, is non-GMO and is Paleo friendly.

One serving (about 30 grams) provides about 20 grams of protein and approximately 120 calories. It contains between 0 to 2 grams of sugar and between 1 to 3 grams of carbs, depending on the flavor and features calcium, iron and potassium. Organic Bone Broth Protein is also a great choice for people with sensitivities to dairy, grains, gluten, peas, soy and nuts.

Depending on how you plan to use it, you can try a number of different flavors. Organic Bone Broth Protein comes in a variety of flavors, both sweet and savory, including: vanilla, chocolate, peanut butter, savory herbs, sweet greens and café mocha. It makes a great addition to soups, stews, casseroles, frittatas, smoothies, pancakes and muffins; it can also be simply mixed with hot water to make a fast cup of bone broth.

MY BONE BROTH PROTEIN EXPERIENCE

II I replaced my old protein powder with Bone Broth Protein Pure in my morning smoothies, and noticed significant changes in my energy and stamina throughout the day! This is a product I don't want to live without. II

– Shelly C.

COLLAGEN SUPPLEMENTS: A PRODUCT OVERVIEW

	Collagen Type(s) and Nutrients	Flavors	Grams of Protein per Serving	Benefits
Multi Collagen Protein	Types I, II, III, V, X	Unflavored Vanilla Chocolate Strawberry Lemonade Cucumber Lime Cold Brew Beauty Within Beauty + Sleep	7-10	Supports joint comfort and flexibility[†] Supports bone health[†] Supports healthy skin, hair and nails[†] Supports a health weight and restful sleep[†]
Bone Broth Collagen	Types I, II, III, X Glucosamine Chondroitin Hyaluronic acid	Pure Vanilla Chocolate	10	Supports healthy digestion[†] Supports healthy immune system function[†] Supports healthy skin, hair and nails[†] Clinically shown to support joint comfort, flexibility and cartilage health[†]
Organic Bone Broth Collagen	Types I, II, III, X Glucosamine Chondroitin Hyaluronic acid	Pure Vanilla Chocolate	10	Supports healthy digestion[†] Supports healthy immune system function[†] Supports healthy skin, hair and nails[†] Clinically shown to support joint comfort, flexibility and cartilage health[†]
KetoCOLLAGEN	Types I, II, V MCT oil powder	Unflavored	15	Supports healthy skin[†] Supports healthy joints[†] Supports healthy gut[†]
Bone Broth Protein	Type II Glucosamine Chondroitin Hyaluronic acid	Pure Vanilla Turmeric Chocolate Cinnamon Apple Banana Crème Greens Coffee	20	Supports healthy digestion and immune system function[†] Supports healthy skin[†] Supports healthy joint function[†] Supports muscle building and connective tissue strength[†]
Organic Bone Broth Protein	Type II Glucosamine Chondroitin Hyaluronic acid	French Vanilla Peanut Butter Dark Chocolate Turmeric Spice Cinnamon Apple Banana Crème Greens Cafe Mocha	20	Supports healthy digestion and immune system function[†] Supports healthy skin[†] Supports healthy joint function[†] Supports muscle building and connective tissue strength[†]

[†]These statements have not been evaluated by the Food and Drug Administration. This product is not intended to diagnose, treat, cure or prevent any disease.

THE IMPORTANCE OF EATING A HEALTHY, WELL-ROUNDED DIET

As you'll discover in the next chapter, eating a nutrient-dense diet that includes lots of antioxidants is helpful for maintaining higher collagen levels. That's because a healthy, whole foods-based diet has been shown to support a healthy inflammation response and fight free radical damage (also called oxidative stress), both of which deplete collagen by adding stress to your body.

To help you absorb and utilize more of the collagen you're consuming from both food sources and supplements, you should aim to include a variety of whole foods in your meals, including: fresh vegetables (such as leafy greens, broccoli, cauliflower, asparagus, carrots and bell peppers), fruits (especially those high in vitamin C such as citrus fruits and berries), quality protein-rich foods and healthy fats (such as coconut oil, olive oil, avocado, nuts and seeds). A varied diet that includes enough healthy plant and animal foods will provide your body with the essential nutrients (such as vitamin A, vitamin C, copper and iron) it needs to properly absorb collagen.

CHAPTER 5

COLLAGEN BOOSTERS

Recently, the benefits of collagen have become more widely known, and, accordingly, all types of "natural" collagen-boosting products are now available — including protein powders, supplements, face lotions, serums and even gummy candies made with gelatin. But which of these approaches and/or products, if any, actually work to support increased levels of collagen in your body? Do you really need them, or can you get enough collagen by consuming the foods we discussed in the previous chapter?

To really boost the level of collagen in your body, this two-prong approach is going to be most effective:

1 First, you need to **reduce free radical damage and support a healthy whole-body inflammation response** in order to protect the collagen your body makes on its own. Collagen is susceptible to oxygen free radicals and fragmentation caused by normal aging and unhealthy habits, therefore making some healthy lifestyle changes — such as adding high-antioxidant foods to your diet and exercising appropriately — may really help reduce or eliminate these causes of collagen loss.[1]

2 Second, you not only need to eat more collagen-rich foods but also **increase your consumption of collagen-boosting foods**, which contain specific nutrients and beneficial compounds that help with synthesis and absorption of collagen. There's a good deal of evidence that eating a nutrient-dense diet — one that includes lots of fresh plant foods and high-quality protein sources — can help increase your body's own production of collagen.[2] Remember that because collagen production typically declines with age, eating a healthy diet becomes more important than ever as you reach your 40s, 50s and beyond. Try to focus on eating foods high in the building blocks of collagen (amino acids), in addition to supportive micronutrients like sulfur, copper, vitamin A, vitamin C and B vitamins.

TOP 5 COLLAGEN-BOOSTING FOOD CATEGORIES

Here's an overview of the top collagen-boosting food categories to focus on regularly incorporating into your diet:

High Antioxidant Foods

First and foremost, you want to include a variety of antioxidants in your diet to both help with collagen synthesis and to aid in preventing excess collagen loss. In animal studies, antioxidant status has been shown to increase collagen content and to reduce the dangerous effects of collagen loss.[3] Antioxidants are found in unprocessed plant foods, especially those that are brightly colored (such as orange, yellow, red and green foods). In fact, a study showed that the antioxidant lycopene, found abundantly in tomatoes, can help prevent collagen breakdown in humans and even aid in protecting skin from sun damage.[4]

Collagen-Rich Foods vs. Collagen-Boosting Foods

You may be wondering why you need to eat both collagen-rich foods and collagen-boosting foods. As you make your way through this chapter, remember that consuming collagen-boosting foods, herbs and spices will not only aid your body with collagen synthesis, but also support the absorption of the collagen you consume. In short, by supporting your collagen-rich diet with collagen-boosting foods and more, you're helping your body get the most out of *Multi Collagen Makeover*. It's a win-win!.

So, what types of foods provide the most antioxidants? Examples include:

- Fruits such as berries (such as açaí, maqui and goji), kiwi, apples, citrus fruits and avocados.

- Vegetables such as carrots, butternut squash, sweet potatoes, leafy greens, onions, tomatoes, bell peppers, eggplant, asparagus, broccoli, Brussels sprouts and other cruciferous veggies.

- Dietary "superfoods" such as green tea (including matcha), raw cocoa, gooseberry, maca powder, spirulina, chlorella and beneficial mushrooms (see Top Collagen-Boosting Herbs and Spices on page 70 for more information on beneficial mushrooms).

Want a great time-saving strategy for consuming more of these nutrient-dense foods every day? Try juicing them or adding them to smoothies. For example, you can make a raw green juice with kale, carrots and apple, or a smoothie with berries and spinach. See Chapter 6 for specific juicing recommendations and Chapter 7 for some of our most loved smoothie recipes.

Sulfur-Rich Foods

Sulfur is an essential micronutrient and another critical component involved in making collagen. In the body, proteins that are particularly high in sulfur include collagen and keratin, both of which provide structure to your skin and other tissues.[5] Sulfur is the third most abundant mineral, based on percentage of total body weight, and a component of amino acids, including methionine, cysteine, cystine and homocysteine.[6] It also aids in the production of glutathione, which is considered a key antioxidant.

Foods rich in sulfur include high-protein foods like meat, fish and eggs. To a lesser extent, sulfur compounds are found in certain plant foods such as broccoli, cauliflower, garlic, onions, nuts and legumes. How much sulfur do you need? Most experts recommend that adults get between 800 to 900 milligrams per day, and up to 1,500 milligrams per day to provide joint and tissue support.

Fermented Vegetables

Fermented or cultured veggies, such as kimchi, sauerkraut and real pickles, are traditional foods that provide probiotics and other benefits. Fermenting vegetables is also a great way to preserve them for a longer period of time, which is why they have been a part of ancestral diets for centuries. Not only do fermented veggies provide antioxidants, fiber and vitamins and minerals (such as vitamins A, C and more), but they also have benefits such as promoting digestive health and supporting healthy cholesterol levels. One of the greatest things about fermented veggies is that the fermentation of natural sugars found in plants increases probiotic lactic acid bacteria (LAB), which can support the digestive system and gut health.[7]

Omega-3 Fatty Acid Foods

Omega-3 fatty acids have health-promoting properties that benefit just about every part of your body, especially your heart and central nervous system. The best sources of omega-3s include wild-caught fish such as salmon, sardines, mackerel, halibut and tuna. You can also take omega-3 fish oil supplements to boost your intake if you don't regularly eat fish two to three times per week.

In addition to supporting a healthy inflammation response, omega-3s have also been shown to help promote skin hydration and support both mental and cardiovascular health. They are necessary for growth and development as well as healthy aging.[8]

Collagen Busters: *Don't* Do This!

Now that you know which foods help boost your collagen production, let's consider the types of things you should *not* be doing — things that can speed up the loss of collagen. As you review this list, keep in mind that poor lifestyle and dietary habits contribute to oxidative stress, also called free radical damage, which depletes collagen. Essentially, anything that "ages" you more quickly also depletes your collagen stores.

Here are the most important habits and dietary choices to avoid in order to prevent accelerated loss of collagen:

- Eating inflammatory, packaged foods, especially those made with added sugar, white flour and refined vegetable oils or trans-fats.

- Eating a nutrient-poor diet, which can result in developing nutrient deficiencies, such as in B vitamins, zinc, selenium or electrolytes (such as magnesium and potassium).

- Over-exercising without allowing for enough recovery.

- Smoking and consuming too much alcohol.

- Experiencing toxin exposure.

- Depriving yourself of sleep.

- Having excessive sunlight exposure that damages your skin.

TOP COLLAGEN-BOOSTING HERBS AND SPICES

Many herbs and spices, both dried and fresh, have antioxidant and immune-supportive effects that may help prevent loss or degradation of collagen. Here are the top culinary and tonic herbs and spices:

Culinary Herbs and Spices

Herbs and spices that help boost collagen include: turmeric, ginger, rosemary, parsley, thyme, sage, oregano, cayenne, black pepper, basil, mint and cinnamon. These contain beneficial compounds, including phenolic diterpenes, phenolic carboxylic acids and biphenyls. Additionally, these herbs and spices contain flavonoids that are involved in antioxidant defenses, a healthy inflammation response and cell renewal.[12] Use these liberally when you cook to add flavor to your meals without relying on too much sugar or salt.

You can also get creative by making herbal infusions (see Chapter 6 for more information) or by adding some herbs to fresh green juices, tea or water.

If you choose to make homemade bone broth, definitely consider adding several types of herbs to increase the antioxidant content. For example, turmeric, parsley, thyme, bay leaf, ginger and peppercorn all make great additions to broth or stock.

Tonic Herbs

In addition to consuming culinary herbs and spices, supplementing with adaptogen herbs, tonic herbs and other supplements that are found in capsule or powder form can also slow loss of collagen.[13]

Ashwagandha is a valuable herb for helping to reduce the effects of stress and free radical damage on the body. In animal studies, it has been shown to offer protection against the production of autoantibodies and support joint health and other bodily functions related to loss of collagen.

Other adaptogen herbs used for the same purpose in ancient healthcare systems, such as Ayurveda and Traditional Chinese Herbalism, include: mushrooms, Indian gooseberry, American or Asian ginseng, astralagus and rhodiola. Mushrooms possess antioxidant and microbial-balancing properties, which is why they have been used to support a wide variety of body systems for centuries. Based on findings in both human and animal studies, beneficial mushrooms may help offer protection against collagen degradation and help promote collagen synthesis involved in normal wound healing.[14]

Types of mushrooms that have been shown to have powerful and functional properties include: *Lentinus, Auricularia. Hericium, Grifola, Flammulina, Sparassis crispa, Pleurotus* and *Tremella.* In one study, oral administration of *Sparassis crispa* (or SC, a mushroom sometimes called Cauliflower Mushroom) showed positive effects in supporting already-healthy blood sugar levels. SC was shown to increase in the migration of macrophages and fibroblasts and to increase synthesis of type I collagen.[15] Other studies have found that bioactive polysaccharides from mushrooms play a key role in immunomodulation, maturation, differentiation or proliferation of cells involved in host defense mechanisms and tissue repair. One study found that oral administration of proteoglycan isolated from *Phellinus linteus* (sometimes called Black Hoof Mushroom) helped support joint health in humans.[16]

TOP 5 COLLAGEN-BOOSTING VITAMINS AND MINERALS

Eating a well-rounded diet will help provide you with many vitamins and minerals that aid in cooling inflammation and benefit your body as a whole. However, there are certain vitamins that you may want to consider also using in supplement form. The following vitamins and minerals have strong antioxidant properties and may help boost your collagen production.

Vitamin C

Research has shown that vitamin C is one of the most important vitamins for supporting the synthesis of collagen. Vitamin C is a natural antioxidant that has, immune-supportive and photoprotective properties, in addition to facilitating the production of key enzymes that are involved in collagen biosynthesis.[16] In studies on adult women and men (ranging from their 20s to 70s), vitamin C has been show to help induce significant collagen synthesis in all age groups with minimal side effects.[17] Vitamin C can be found in foods such as citrus fruits, camu camu, kiwi, papaya, guava, leafy green vegetables like spinach or kale, cruciferous veggies, bell peppers, berries and tropical fruits. It can also be taken in supplement form to boost overall vitamin C status and support healthy immune function. The recommended daily allowance for vitamin C is 90 milligrams for men age 19 and older and 75 milligrams for women age 19 and older.

Vitamin A

Vitamin A has been shown to help scavenge free radicals, which can damage tissue and contribute to accelerated aging. It has also been shown to help decrease photoaging (the premature aging of skin due to sun exposure), caused in part by increased elaboration of collagen-degrading matrix and reduced collagen synthesis.[18] Plant-derived sources of vitamin A (such as carrots, winter squash, broccoli and spinach) have been shown to support multiple facets of skin health.

Vitamin B$_6$ (Pyridoxine)

Roughly 10 percent of people will develop kidney stones at some point, due to their diet, genetics and/or lifestyle factors. If you have a history of kidney stones or trouble digesting protein due to oxalate accumulation, vitamin B6 actually may be able to help you absorb collagen more safely and effectively. Interestingly, gelatin and collagen contain an amino acid called hydroxyproline, which can increase urinary excretion of oxalates. Additionally, in animal studies, a deficiency in vitamin B6 has been linked with poor collagen production, suggesting that vitamin B6 sufficiency may help support proper collagen production.[19]

You need adequate vitamin B6 to metabolize amino acids, in addition to other nutrients.[20] Consuming more vitamin B6 may help with this process. In addition to preventing vitamin B$_6$ deficiency, it's also important to stay hydrated to support kidney health, especially if you eat a high-protein diet. If you do have vitamin B6 deficiency or a high risk for developing kidney stones, you can supplement with 5 to 30 milligrams of vitamin B6 daily (or even more under the care of a doctor). Supplementing with pure glycine rather than collagen protein is another option for people dealing with kidney issues, since glycine is very unlikely to contribute to stone formation.

MY BONE BROTH COLLAGEN EXPERIENCE

❚❚ I feel a huge difference in my joint flexibility and mobility ... I also notice that my skin is clearer. Also, my hair looks healthy and shiny. I will take Bone Broth Collagen for the rest of my life. ❚❚

— Julie V.

Biotin (Vitamin B$_7$)

Collagen and biotin work together synergistically to help promote healthy skin and strong hair and nails. Biotin plays a role in fatty acid metabolism and cell growth, and consuming it has been shown to help reduce hair loss and nail brittleness in adults who are deficient. The best sources for biotin include: egg yolks, liver, cheese, salmon, avocados and berries. The recommended daily allowance of biotin for adults over 19 years old is 30 micrograms.

Copper

Copper is needed for key enzymatic reactions involved in collagen synthesis, including the enzyme lysyl oxidase. This mineral forms the basis of the crosslinking of collagen and elastin, helps with stabilization of collagen fibrils and supports healthy connective tissues, such as those in the heart, blood vessels and bones.[21] Nuts, seeds, organ meats and 100-percent whole grains are all good dietary sources of copper. The recommended daily allowance of copper for adults (both men and women) is 900 µg, or .9 milligrams.

BOOSTING YOUR COLLAGEN WITH ESSENTIAL OILS

Essential oils are plant-derived volatile oils that contain concentrated amounts of active constituents. Simply put, essential oils are so amazing because of their ability to naturally support a healthy inflammation response, support joint health, boost skin health, promote relaxation, support healthy digestion and more. Certain essential oils have microbial-balancing, calming and/or energizing effects.[23] Examples of popular essential oils include frankincense, peppermint and lavender oil.

To help reduce free radical damage and promote collagen production, some of the most beneficial essential oils include: frankincense, tea tree, ginger, geranium, cinnamon, calendula, neroli, lemon, grapefruit and oregano.

Each oil has its own special properties and uses, such as frankincense supporting the immune system, tea tree supporting skin health and oregano supporting digestive health. Lemon, tea tree, calendula, neroli, lavender and geranium essential oils can be used on the skin to help boost elasticity and hydration. Combine these essential oils with a carrier oil, such as jojoba or coconut oil, before applying the blend to your skin.

Essential oils can also be diffused, vaporized and inhaled, and some can be taken internally (only if the oil is 100 percent pure and therapeutic grade). Taking 1 to 2 drops of pure frankincense, lemon or oregano internally has been shown to help support healthy immune function and gut health.[24] In fact, a 2014 study found that oregano oil has powerful microbial balancing benefits.[25]

What About Exercise?

Exercise is one of the ultimate collagen boosters, due to how it helps promote collagen uptake in the muscles, tendons and joints. Studies have found that taking collagen orally before exercising helps tendons to absorb and utilize amino acids best. Recent research suggests that taking 10 to 15 grams of collagen protein about 30 minutes before exercising can help support tendon health, facilitate muscle repair and growth and even support joint health.[22]

BOOSTING YOUR COLLAGEN WITH TOPICAL APPLICATIONS

Collagen is commonly used in combination with other compounds to help protect and smooth the skin, especially by those looking to improve the appearance of fine lines. Here are some of the most popular topical applications:

Indian Gooseberry

In animal studies, Indian gooseberry (*Phyllanthus emblica*, a fruit native to southeast Asia) has been shown to promote type I collagen. One animal study found that at a concentration of 0.1 milligram/ milliliter, Indian gooseberry extract used topically significantly increased type I pro-collagen levels in the treated group of mice by up to 6.78-fold greater than the untreated control group of mice.[26] The authors concluded: "In summary, emblica extract has a promising pharmacological effect that benefits collagen synthesis and protects against its degradation and could be used as a natural anti-aging ingredient." *Phyllanthus emblica* (trade named Emblica) has also been found to have long-lasting and broad-spectrum antioxidant activity, another reason it may boost skin health.[27] Aside from using gooseberry extract on your skin, you can also look for edible Indian gooseberry in dried or powder form at health food stores and online retailers.

Retinol

One compound found in many topical anti-aging products is vitamin A (retinol), usually at concentrations of about 1 percent. Studies have found that applying vitamin A to the skin daily helps increase fibroblast growth and collagen synthesis and reduces collagen-degrading.[28] This is beneficial for not only improving the appearance of aged, sun-damaged skin but also for helping to fight wrinkles, lines and sagging in sun-protected, younger skin.

Hyaluronic Acid

Hyaluronic acid (HA) supports skin texture and appearance, and it even supports joint health. HA is a lubricating, clear substance that's produced by the body naturally and found in the greatest concentrations in the skin, joints and eye sockets. It helps retain collagen, increases moisture by absorbing large amounts of water and supports your skin's elasticity and flexibility. HA can be found in creams, serums and lotions, or it can be administered by dermatologists via injections. A topical application of serum containing around 0.1 percent HA has been shown to help support skin hydration, aid in reducing wrinkle appearance and promote elasticity.

All-Natural Applications

Other than plant extracts derived from essential oils, natural ingredients that can help naturally support skin health include:[29,30,31]

- Raw honey

- Colloidal oatmeal

- Pomegranate extract

- Aloe vera

- Coconut or olive oil

- Green and black tea

- Raw shea butter

- Argan oil

CHAPTER 6

THE MULTI COLLAGEN
MAKEOVER PLAN

The program detailed in this chapter provides guidelines on how to follow a three-day cleanse and a 28-day collagen-loading plan. You'll learn exactly how to use collagen foods and supplements as part of an overall healthy lifestyle that will help you reach your goals and maintain success thereafter.

This plan is ideal for those who have been lacking adequate collagen for some time. Remember, the goal is to balance your intake of amino acids (the building blocks of proteins). This can be accomplished by eating a variety of high-protein foods, especially those that supply collagen and help your body regenerate, in addition to superfoods that provide key vitamins, minerals and antioxidants. As you begin this plan, just remember that your main focus should be to get a minimum of three servings of collagen each day.

While the dietary suggestions in this program may be a departure from the way you're currently eating, remember that this can be a good, health-promoting change. Following this collagen-loading plan will help overhaul your diet and allow you to see results quickly — both in terms of healthy weight management (if this is one of your goals) and your overall health. Keep in mind that while this plan might be challenging at the start, as time goes on, you can customize the plan to better fit your needs and preferences.

Also, don't forget to let us know how you're doing! Take a photo before you begin the plan and keep track of your progress (how you're feeling, improvements you're seeing, etc.). Make sure to take an "after" photo as well, and share it with us on Instagram at @ancientnutrition.

THE MULTI COLLAGEN MAKEOVER PLAN OVERVIEW

While you'll find a comprehensive listing of collagen-containing and collagen-boosting foods in the shopping list at the end of this chapter, here is an overview of the approved foods by category:

Proteins

As we discussed in Chapter 1, protein in your diet is important for numerous reasons: It helps to fight cravings and supports healthy muscle mass, assist the normal regeneration of tissue and support a healthy metabolism. Examples of healthy protein sources include: grass-fed beef, lamb or venison, pasture-raised chicken or turkey, wild-caught fish, pasture-raised eggs, raw/fermented dairy products and protein powders containing collagen and/or bone broth.

Depending on the specific diet you follow, you should aim to get 25 to 35 percent or more of your daily calories from protein. Keep in mind that sea-based proteins are best when wild-caught, and land-based proteins are best when grass-fed, free-range and/or organic. We recommend avoiding pork and shellfish, as they may contain high levels of toxins. Organic and/or grass-fed dairy is best, such as cheeses made from organic sheep or goat milk.

If possible, have a protein source with every meal, aiming to get about 20 to 30 grams of protein from each of your main meals. If you're a vegetarian or vegan, be sure to eat the recommended daily amount of seeds or nuts for a good protein source. If you use protein powders, always read the labels and be sure the powder is not sweetened with sugars or any sweetener other than natural stevia or monk fruit.

Fats and Oils

Healthy fats should be included in your diet every day, as they help support nutrient absorption, appetite control, hormone production and mental health. Examples of healthy fats and oils include: virgin coconut oil and olive oil, grass-fed butter, ghee, avocado and avocado oil, nuts, seeds and organic mayonnaise. Depending on the specific diet you follow, you should get about 30 percent or more of your daily calories from healthy fats (sometimes much more if you follow a low-carb or ketogenic diet). Spread fat consumption throughout your day, aiming to have some with every meal. When purchasing fats and oils for this program, select organic, high-quality products whenever possible. Do not cook with extra virgin olive oil (use coconut oil or butter); instead, use it as a salad dressing, drizzle it over cooked veggies, or add some to dips and spreads.

Vegetables

You should aim to eat about three to five servings of fresh vegetables daily (each serving is about one cup) in order to support fiber, vitamins and antioxidants intake. Non-starchy veggies (such as leafy greens, peppers, mushrooms, onions, carrots, tomatoes and green beans) are filling and very low in calories. Eat a variety of different types throughout the week; examples include: salads, veggie-based soups, green smoothies and steamed or roasted veggies.

Vegetables can be consumed raw or prepared grilled, steamed or sautéed in an approved fat or oil. Cook your veggies in bone broth (ideal for collagen support) or a bit of butter, ghee or coconut oil. You can make them taste great by drizzling them with extra virgin olive oil, avocado oil or flax seed oil and adding collagen-boosting herbs and spices. Non-starchy veggies should be your biggest source, but starchy veggies like sweet potatoes, yams, beets and butternut squash are also good choices (in smaller amounts) due to their high nutrient content. Stick to having about ½ to one cup of starchy veggies daily, and cook them by roasting (in coconut oil), baking or steaming them and top with grass-fed butter or olive oil.

Fruits

Fresh fruits are great sources of antioxidants, fiber, electrolytes and essential vitamins that help with collagen production and synthesis. Consume about one to three servings of fresh fruit daily (a serving is about ½ cup). Emphasize fruits high in vitamin C, such as oranges, grapefruit, kiwi, papaya, mango, guava and all types of berries. Berries (like blueberries, cranberries, raspberries and blackberries) are especially beneficial because they're low in sugar but a great source of fiber, vitamin C and antioxidants such as phenolic acids and flavonoids.[1] Add fruits to fresh-squeezed juices, smoothies, salads, yogurt or eat them in their natural form as a dessert.

Fermented Foods

Try to eat fermented foods daily to help support digestion and gut health. Remember, fermented foods include sauerkraut, kimchi, fermented assorted veggies, raw apple cider vinegar (ACV) and raw coconut vinegar. Eat these on their own, serve them on top of salads or with meat or eggs or make salad dressings with ACV.

Grains and Legumes

We recommend eating beans and legumes and 100 percent whole or ancient grains in moderation. Examples of healthy legumes and grains include: chickpeas, black beans, kidney beans, quinoa, black or brown rice, gluten-free oats and buckwheat.

To support digestion and a healthy weight, stick to having about ½ to one cup of cooked grains and legumes daily. It's best to soak and sprout legumes and grains before cooking them to help make them easier to digest and to release their nutrients. We also recommend cooking grains and legumes in bone broth in order to help increase their nutrient density. If you'll be including bread in your diet, look for sprouted/flourless grain bread (avoid bread and other grain products made with white/enriched flour).

Seasonings and Herbs

Seasonings and herbs should be consumed daily, if possible, either fresh or as dry herbs and spices. Use these liberally to flavor your meals without adding sugar, processed oils or extra calories. Ingredients to avoid when purchasing seasonings include: monosodium glutamate (MSG), glutamic acid, natural flavorings, sugar and dextrose. Some seasonings and herbs to incorporate in recipes include: vinegars, basil, garlic powder, hot peppers, oregano, thyme and more.

Sweeteners

Read labels carefully to avoid consuming products that contain added sugar. Skip any product that lists sugar or artificial sweeteners, including under the names fructose, sucrose, acesulfame potassium, aspartame, saccharin and sucralose. Instead of adding white sugar to recipes, sweeten foods lightly with stevia extract, raw honey or monk fruit (in moderation). You can also use whole or puréed fruit to sweeten anything from smoothies and yogurt to oatmeal and baked goods.

Beverages

Stay hydrated throughout the day by drinking plain water, bone broth, herbal tea (see Herbal Teas and Infusions), raw juices and organic coffee (in moderation). If you drink coffee or alcohol, make sure to consume extra water to prevent dehydration. Freshly squeezed lemon and lime are delicious natural additives for beverages. You can also flavor your water by adding organic or pure essential oils, including lemon, orange, grapefruit, peppermint and cinnamon. Other approved beverages include: coconut milk, unsweetened almond milk, green tea, black tea and seltzer water. Read labels carefully when buying bottled beverages and avoid any that contain added sugar. Whenever possible, make your own fresh veggie or fruit juice, rather than buying bottled juice.

Herbal Teas and Infusions

When it comes to making sure you're consuming enough collagen-boosting herbs and spices, drinking herbal teas and infusions can be a great way to make sure you're staying on track. Here are some quick tips on how to make your own herbal teas and infusions.

Herbal Teas

Drinking herbal tea is a great way to get the many immune-supportive, digestion-promoting properties of herbs every day. You can make herbal tea at home by steeping one tablespoon of herbs of your choice (such as ginger root, turmeric, mint, etc.) in hot water for 5 to 10 minutes. Ginger tea is great to drink after dinner to help with digestion, while peppermint tea aids in curbing cravings while fasting or between meals. You can also purchase herbal teas such as echinacea or chamomile in stores. Echinacea is a popular herbal tea for supporting the immune system, and chamomile is known for boosting relaxation and restful sleep. You can have several cups of herbal tea daily, especially since it's caffeine-free and helps to keep you hydrated.

Herbal Infusions

You're likely familiar with herbal teas, but what are herbal infusions? Herbal infusions are similar to herbal teas but stronger than teas because they require a larger quantity of herbs. To make your own herbal infusion, steep a cup of herbs of your choice in water for about seven hours. This amount of time allows for more of the herbs' beneficial compounds to be released into the liquid. Keep the infusion in an air-tight jar and drink it cold or heated within several days. Because the infusions are strong, it's recommended that you don't drink more than one cup a day.

Herbs to use in teas and infusions include ...

Cinnamon Bark

Sage

Burdock Root

Licorice Root

Thyme

Cilantro

Ginger

Turmeric

Chamomile

Echinacea

Mint

Rosemary

Parsley

Oregano

Lavender

THE MULTI COLLAGEN MAKEOVER PLAN

The Multi Collagen Makeover Plan will last a total of 31 days and is broken up into two distinct phases — a three-day cleanse and a 28-day meal plan. Here's an overview of what you can expect:

The Three-Day Collagen Cleanse. The first three days of this meal plan will be a "collagen cleanse." You'll be consuming a liquid diet for three days that includes a combination of bone broth (homemade or supplement powder), raw juices, coffee, tea, herbal infusions and collagen shakes/smoothies.

The 28-Day Multi Collagen Makeover Meal Plan. The following 28 days will include:

- **Optional Cleanse Day.** The following 28 days will include one optional day of cleansing each week (we like to refer to this as "Cleanse Day Wednesday").

- **Plentiful Lunches and Dinners.** The structure of every other day of the program will be similar. You will have liquids for breakfast (such as collagen-boosting smoothies, tea/herbal infusion, coffee, broth, etc.) and have delicious, healthy, satisfying meals for lunch and dinner. This is a form of intermittent fasting, or daily cleansing, that will catapult detoxification and has been shown to help support healthy weight loss, if desired (we'll discuss the benefits of intermittent fasting more in the following pages).

- **Desserts.** Two nights each week, you'll have the option to eat dessert. While they taste great, the dessert recipes included in this meal plan and in the following chapter still include collagen and other beneficial ingredients to keep you on track.

- **Snacks.** To help keep you satisfied, you'll also have the option to eat snacks. If you find yourself needing snacks throughout the day due to hunger, such as if you're very active, then you'll find healthy snack recommendations in the sample meal plan on the following pages and snack recipes in Chapter 7.

The Three-Day Collagen Cleanse

During the three-day collagen cleanse, you'll adhere to the following guidelines:

- Consume only liquids for all meals, which can include bone broth, raw juice, teas, herbal infusions, coffee and water. (For more information on why you'll be avoiding solid foods during this cleanse, see The Beneficial Impacts of Intermittent Fasting.)

- Aim to consume **at least three servings of collagen each day.** You'll get collagen from drinking real bone broth (homemade or store-bought) or using Multi Collagen Protein, Bone Broth Collagen, KetoCOLLAGEN or Bone Broth Protein in recipes — or a combination of these. A serving of bone broth is one cup (8 ounces), while a serving (one scoop) of Multi Collagen Protein is approximately 7 to 10 grams (provides about 7 grams of protein), a serving (one scoop) of Bone Broth Collagen is about 15 grams (provides about 13 grams of protein) and a serving (one scoop) of Bone Broth Protein is between 22 to 29 grams (provides about 20 grams of protein).

- Consume three servings of herbal tea/herbal infusions each day (each serving is about one cup, or 8 ounces).

- To help increase your antioxidant intake, consume two servings of raw juices each day (each serving is about 4 to 8 ounces).

The Beneficial Impacts of Intermittent Fasting

In conjunction with the guidelines above, you'll avoid eating solid foods during these three days, as you'll be practicing intermittent fasting. We've included intermittent fasting in The Multi Collagen Makeover Plan because it has been shown to help promote healthy weight loss, support cardiovascular health, support already-healthy blood sugar levels, promote cognitive functioning and support a healthy inflammation response.[2,3,4] In fact, "voluntary abstinence from food" (fasting) has been practiced since before the time of written history by people living around the globe. There are several different styles of fasting, but all have one thing in common: They promote beneficial hormonal and metabolic adaptations that help protect against imbalance of blood sugar and metabolism.[5]

Today, intermittent fasting is considered to be a feasible and sustainable strategy for promoting metabolic health, including helping with weight loss.[6] Intermittent fasting can result in increased fat burning and healthy weight loss by forcing your body to use up fat stores as fuel. Because you'll be avoiding solid foods while you fast, this will also reduce the amount of stress placed on your digestive system and may help with detoxification. Recently, studies have even shown that intermittent fasting (such as alternate-day fasting) or short-term repeated fasting may increase the life span of animals.[7]

To get the most from intermittent fasting, you'll be consuming easy-to-digest whole foods in liquid form in order to squeeze as many nutrients as possible into your day. The liquids you consume during the cleanse will provide essential nutrients, help to decrease hunger and help to keep you hydrated. Because you'll be consuming collagen several times per day, you should experience less muscle loss than typically occurs while dieting or fasting, due to a higher intake of amino acids, such as glycine and proline, that help maintain muscle tissue.

During your cleanse, keep this in mind: While intermittent fasting has loads of benefits, always still listen to your body. If you feel weakness or fatigue, consider increasing your intake a bit and have a light meal or snack.

Jumpstart Your Cleanse with Juice

Why is juicing an important part of the Three-Day Collagen Cleanse? Simply put, juicing is an easy way to get a whopping heap of fresh veggies, herbs and fruit into your diet in one easy shot. Because they provide nutrients in liquid form, juices are easy to digest. As a result, your body absorbs more nutrients (such as vitamins A, C and E found in fruits and veggies) quickly.

Drinking raw, fresh-made juice can increase your intake of antioxidants and nutrients such as chlorophyll, a green pigment found in certain plant foods that is beneficial for detoxification and healthy inflammation support. Juices (especially those made with a variety of different vegetables) have been shown to increase intake of polyphenols and vitamins, and studies have found that fruit and vegetable juices positively affect metabolic and cardiovascular health.

The best and easiest way to make homemade raw juices is with a juicer; however, you can blend ingredients in a high-speed blender and then strain out the solid pulp as a back-up method. To save time, make at least two servings of juice at once, and consume the leftovers (stored air-tight in the refrigerator) within two days. While consuming fresh/raw juice is recommended, you can mix water with a green superfood powder formula to make a juice quickly and easily, if you're in a pinch.

We'll provide some great, nutrient-packed juice recipe ideas in the Three-Day Collagen Cleanse beginning on the next page. If you'd like to experiment with making your own juice, though, we recommend using these veggies, herbs and fruit due to their alkalizing, detoxifying and/or collagen-boosting properties: beets, carrots, ginger, lemon juice, cucumbers, cabbage, spinach, blackberries, kiwi, papaya, guava, raspberries, parsley, cilantro, mint, milk thistle, kale, Swiss chard, wheatgrass, romaine lettuce and Brussels sprouts.

THE THREE-DAY COLLAGEN CLEANSE AT-A-GLANCE

Here's a sample overview of your three-day cleanse. (Note: Meals appearing in italics refer to *Multi Collagen Makeover* recipes in Chapter 7.)

DAY 1

Upon Waking

- 1 scoop of Multi Collagen Protein, Bone Broth Protein or Organic Bone Broth Protein mixed with a glass of water, almond milk or unsweetened coconut milk

Morning/Mid-Morning

- *Cherry Vanilla Collagen Smoothie* (page 112)
- Coffee or herbal tea of your choice (optional)
- Herbal infusion of your choice

Lunch/Mid-Day

- Orange Veggie Juice: 6 carrots, 1 orange, 1 knob ginger and 1 cucumber

Snack/Afternoon

- Herbal infusion/tea of your choice
- 1 scoop of Multi Collagen Protein mixed with a glass of water, almond milk or unsweetened coconut milk (optional)

Dinner/Night

- Whole Body Tonic Juice: 4 celery stalks, ½ cucumber, 1 cup pineapple, ½ green apple, 1 cup spinach, 1 lemon and 1 knob ginger.
- *Carrot Ginger Bone Broth Shake* (page 111)
- Herbal infusion/tea of your choice

Before Bed

- 1 scoop of Multi Collagen Protein Beauty + Sleep (or flavor of your choice) mixed with a glass of water, almond milk or unsweetened coconut milk

DAY 2

Upon Waking

- 1 scoop of Multi Collagen Protein, Bone Broth Protein or Organic Bone Broth Protein mixed with a glass of water, almond milk or unsweetened coconut milk

Morning/Mid-Morning

- *Strawberry Coconut Bone Broth Smoothie* (page 118)
- Coffee or herbal tea of your choice (optional)
- Herbal infusion of your choice

Lunch/Mid-Day

- Bone-Building Juice: ½ avocado, 2 cups spinach, 1 cup cabbage and 2 cucumbers
- Serving of bone broth (homemade or using Bone Broth Protein)

Snack/Afternoon

- Herbal infusion/tea of your choice
- 1 scoop of Bone Broth Protein mixed with a glass of water, almond milk or unsweetened coconut milk (optional)

Dinner/Night

- Spicy Heart Health Juice: ⅛ or less jalapeño pepper, 1 knob ginger, 1 clove garlic, 1 medium beet, 2 carrots, 1 lemon and 1 cucumber
- Serving of bone broth (homemade or using Bone Broth Protein)
- Herbal infusion/tea of your choice

Before Bed

- 1 scoop of Multi Collagen Protein Beauty + Sleep (or flavor of your choice) mixed with a glass of water, almond milk or unsweetened coconut milk

DAY 3

Upon Waking

- 1 scoop of Multi Collagen Protein, Bone Broth Protein or Organic Bone Broth Protein mixed with a glass of water, almond milk or unsweetened coconut milk

Morning/Mid-Morning

- *Peach Probiotic Smoothie* (page 116)
- Coffee or herbal tea of your choice (optional)
- Herbal infusion of your choice

Lunch/Mid-Day

- Immune-Supporting Juice: 1 bell pepper (red, green, yellow or orange), 1 head/ stem broccoli, 1 lemon, 1 cucumber, 1 knob ginger and 1 tablespoon apple cider vinegar
- Serving of bone broth (homemade or using Bone Broth Protein)

Snack/Afternoon

- Herbal infusion/tea of your choice
- 1 scoop of Multi Collagen Protein mixed with a glass of water, almond milk or unsweetened coconut milk (optional)

Dinner/Night

- Orange Veggie Juice: 6 carrots, 1 orange, 1 knob ginger and 1 cucumber
- *Creamy Tomato Soup* (page 123)
- Herbal infusion/tea of your choice

Before Bed

- 1 scoop of Multi Collagen Protein Beauty + Sleep (or flavor of your choice) mixed with a glass of water, almond milk or unsweetened coconut milk

THE 28-DAY MULTI COLLAGEN MAKEOVER MEAL PLAN

After your initial three-day cleanse, every day that you are not cleansing will be roughly the same. This means that six days per week, you should aim to follow this same basic eating schedule, continuing this over the course of 28 days:

Breakfasts will consist of approved liquids/beverages, which means the beginning of each day will be similar. Depending on the day, your breakfast might include a collagen smoothie, tea/herbal infusion, coffee, broth or other approved beverage.

Lunches and dinners will consist of healthy, solid, balanced meals. You'll be supplied with a wide variety of collagen-filled recipes and meal suggestions. In order to provide the collagen-boosting foods and nutrients described earlier in this book, your meals will include a combination of vegetables, a source of collagen, a source of quality protein, a source of healthy fat and some complex carbs (carbs are optional if you follow a low-carb diet). In the following 28-day meal plan, you'll find specific recommendations for different meals pulled from the recipes featured in Chapter 7 (both liquid-based recipes for breakfast and more filling meals for lunch and dinner). You may choose to follow this sample plan exactly or adapt as needed.

As you navigate the 28-day meal plan, keep in mind that you're working toward the goal of having **the equivalent of three servings (minimum) of collagen each day.** Just as you did during the three-day cleanse, you'll continue to use Multi Collagen Protein, Bone Broth Protein and/or homemade bone broth. Feel free to have a combination of real bone broth and several servings of your favorite collagen protein powders each day to mix things up. Remember that you can also cook a variety of foods (such as grains, legumes or veggies) in bone broth as well as add broth to soup, stews, smoothies and more.

So, let's jump in! Here's an example of what the first seven days of your 28-day meal plan will look like. As a special bonus, you can access an additional week's worth of meal plans at www.ancientnutrition.com/mcmmealplan. **(Note: After the first 14 days, you can choose to repeat the meal plan, swap in your favorite recipes from Chapter 7, incorporate more leftovers or adapt further as desired).** You can also see our Tips for Success at www.ancienutrition.com/mcmtips.

DAY 1

Upon Waking

- 1 scoop of Multi Collagen Protein Cold Brew, Bone Broth Protein or Organic Bone Broth Protein mixed with a glass of water, almond milk or unsweetened coconut milk

Morning/Mid-Morning

- *Cherry Vanilla Collagen Smoothie* (page 112)
- Organic coffee (optional: blended with 1 to 2 tablespoons of coconut oil, butter or ghee) or tea/herbal infusion of your choice

Lunch/Mid-Day

- *Butternut Bisque* (page 122)
- Side salad topped with homemade dressing: 1 tablespoon of olive oil mixed with apple cider vinegar and seasoned to taste
- *Golden Tea* (page 109)

Snack/Afternoon

- *Cauliflower Hummus* (page 142) served with raw veggies
- 1 scoop of Multi Collagen Protein Vanilla (or flavor of your choice) mixed with a glass of water, almond milk or unsweetened coconut milk (optional)

Dinner/Night

- 6 ounces of wild-caught salmon (or another type of wild-caught fish) cooked in 1 tablespoon of coconut or olive oil
- Steamed broccoli or Brussels sprouts, topped with 1 tablespoon of flax oil and seasoned to taste
- ½ baked sweet potato
- Herbal infusion/tea

Before Bed

- 1 scoop of Multi Collagen Protein Beauty + Sleep (or flavor of your choice) mixed with a glass of water, almond milk or unsweetened coconut milk

DAY 2

Upon Waking

- 1 scoop of Multi Collagen Protein, Bone Broth Protein or Organic Bone Broth Protein mixed with a glass of water, almond milk or unsweetened coconut milk

Morning/Mid-Morning

- *Peach Probiotic Smoothie* (page 116)
- Organic coffee (optional: blended with 1 to 2 tablespoons of coconut oil, butter or ghee) or tea/herbal infusion of your choice

Lunch/Mid-Day

- *Indian Curry Soup* (page 124)
- Side salad topped with homemade dressing: 1 tablespoon of olive oil mixed with apple cider vinegar and seasoned to taste
- Herbal infusion/tea

Snack/Afternoon

- 4 ounces of strawberries served with a side of full-fat cottage cheese
- 1 scoop of Multi Collagen Protein Chocolate (or flavor of your choice) mixed with a glass of water, almond milk or unsweetened coconut milk (optional)

Dinner/Night

- *Spaghetti Squash with Roasted Chicken, Lemon and Parsley* (page 128)
- ½ cup of fermented veggies
- Side salad topped with homemade dressing: 1 tablespoon of olive oil mixed with apple cider vinegar and seasoned to taste
- Herbal infusion/tea

Dessert

- *Carrot Cake Squares* (page 149)

Before Bed

- 1 scoop of Multi Collagen Protein Beauty + Sleep (or flavor of your choice) mixed with a glass of water, almond milk or unsweetened coconut milk

DAY 3

Upon Waking

- 1 scoop of Multi Collagen Protein, Bone Broth Protein or Organic Bone Broth Protein mixed with a glass of water, almond milk or unsweetened coconut milk

Morning/Mid-Morning

- *Strawberry Coconut Bone Broth Smoothie* (page 118)
- Organic coffee (optional: blended with 1 to 2 tablespoons of coconut oil, butter or ghee) or tea/herbal infusion of your choice

Lunch/Mid-Day

- *Beef and Butternut Squash Soup* (page 121)
- ½ cup of fermented veggies
- Herbal infusion/tea

Snack/Afternoon

- *Blueberry Muffins* (page 139)
- 1 scoop of Multi Collagen Protein Strawberry Lemonade (or flavor of your choice) mixed with a glass of water, almond milk or unsweetened coconut milk (optional)

Dinner/Night

- *Roasted Chicken with Roma Tomatoes and Onions* (page 127)
- *Maple Glazed Rosemary Carrots* (page 134)
- Herbal infusion/tea

Before Bed

- 1 scoop of Multi Collagen Protein Beauty + Sleep (or flavor of your choice) mixed with a glass of water, almond milk or unsweetened coconut milk

DAY 4 (OPTIONAL CLEANSE DAY)

Upon Waking

- 1 scoop of Multi Collagen Protein Cold Brew, Bone Broth Protein or Organic Bone Broth Protein mixed with a glass of water, almond milk or unsweetened coconut milk

Morning/Mid-Morning

- *Carrot Ginger Bone Broth Shake* (page 111)
- Organic coffee (optional: blended with 1 to 2 tablespoons of coconut oil, butter or ghee) or tea/herbal infusion of your choice

Lunch/Mid-Day

- *Green Brain-Boosting Smoothie* (page 112)
- Organic coffee or herbal tea of your choice (optional)

Snack/Afternoon

- Herbal infusion/tea
- 1 scoop of Multi Collagen Protein Cucumber Lime (or flavor of your choice) mixed with a glass of water, almond milk or unsweetened coconut milk (optional)

Dinner/Night

- Whole Body Tonic Juice: 4 celery stalks, ½ cucumber, 1 cup pineapple, ½ green apple, 1 cup spinach, 1 lemon and 1 knob ginger
- Bone broth soup (or 1 serving of Bone Broth Protein mixed with 1 ¼ cups hot water to make soup)
- Herbal infusion/tea

Before Bed

- 1 scoop of Multi Collagen Protein Beauty + Sleep (or flavor of your choice) mixed with a glass of water, almond milk or unsweetened coconut milk

DAY 5

Upon Waking

- 1 scoop of Multi Collagen Protein, Bone Broth Protein or Organic Bone Broth Protein mixed with a glass of water, almond milk or unsweetened coconut milk

Morning/Mid-Morning

- *Blueberry Bliss Collagen Smoothie* (page 111)
- Organic coffee (optional: blended with 1 to 2 tablespoons of coconut oil, butter or ghee) or tea/herbal infusion of your choice

Lunch/Mid-Day

- *Meatball Soup* (page 125)
- Side salad topped with homemade dressing: 1 tablespoon of olive oil mixed with apple cider vinegar and seasoned to taste
- Herbal infusion/tea

Snack/Afternoon

- *No-Bake Bone Broth Protein Bar* (page 141)
- 1 scoop of Multi Collagen Protein Vanilla (or flavor of your choice) mixed with a glass of water, almond milk or unsweetened coconut milk (optional)

Dinner/Night

- *Quinoa-Stuffed Bell Peppers* (page 129)
- *Strawberry Spinach Salad with Poppy Seed Dressing* (page 136)
- Herbal infusion/tea

Dessert

- *No-Bake Cashew Truffles* (page 151)

Before Bed

- 1 scoop of Multi Collagen Protein Beauty + Sleep (or flavor of your choice) mixed with a glass of water, almond milk or unsweetened coconut milk

DAY 6

Upon Waking

- 1 scoop of Multi Collagen Protein, Bone Broth Protein or Organic Bone Broth Protein mixed with a glass of water, almond milk or unsweetened coconut milk

Morning/Mid-Morning

- *Pumpkin Pie Smoothie* (page 116)
- Organic coffee (optional: blended with 1 to 2 tablespoons of coconut oil, butter or ghee) or tea/herbal infusion of your choice

Lunch/Mid-Day

- *Chicken Tenders* (page 130)
- *Sweet Potato Fries* (page 137)
- Herbal infusion/tea

Snack/Afternoon

- 4 ounces of blueberries served with a side of full-fat cottage cheese
- 1 scoop of Multi Collagen Protein Beauty Within (or flavor of your choice) mixed with a glass of water, almond milk or unsweetened coconut milk (optional)

Dinner/Night

- Leftover *Quinoa-Stuffed Bell Peppers* (page 129)
- *Ghee-Baked Brussels Sprouts* (page 133)
- Herbal infusion/tea

Before Bed

- 1 scoop of Multi Collagen Protein Beauty + Sleep (or flavor of your choice) mixed with a glass of water, almond milk or unsweetened coconut milk

DAY 7

Upon Waking

- 1 scoop of Multi Collagen Protein Cold Brew, Bone Broth Protein or Organic Bone Broth Protein mixed with a glass of water, almond milk or unsweetened coconut milk

Morning/Mid-Morning

- *Green Brain-Boosting Smoothie* (page 112)
- Organic coffee (optional: blended with 1 to 2 tablespoons of coconut oil, butter or ghee) or tea/herbal infusion of your choice

Lunch/Mid-Day

- *"Noodle" Bowls* (page 126)
- Herbal infusion/tea

Snack/Afternoon

- *Kale Chips* (page 145)
- 1 scoop of Bone Broth Protein Chocolate (or flavor of your choice) mixed with a glass of water, almond milk or unsweetened coconut milk (optional)

Dinner/Night

- 6 ounces of organic, free-range chicken cooked in 1 tablespoon of olive or coconut oil
- Summer squash/zucchini sautéed in 1 to 2 teaspoons of oil or ghee
- Herbal infusion/tea

Before Bed

- 1 scoop of Multi Collagen Protein Beauty + Sleep (or flavor of your choice) mixed with a glass of water, almond milk or unsweetened coconut milk

Remember, to access Days 8-14, visit www.ancientnutrition.com/mcmmealplan.

THE MULTI COLLAGEN MAKEOVER FOR LIFE

If you're feeling great after The Multi Collagen Makeover Plan comes to a close, then you can continue to follow the plan's basic guidelines and keep repeating your favorite recipes. Keep focusing on eating whole foods, juicing and fasting (if you find them helpful) and including sources of collagen (such as homemade bone broth, Multi Collagen Protein and Bone Broth Protein) in your daily diet.

However, if you're ready for a change, then you can maintain your momentum by transitioning to a modified plan that still includes plenty of the collagen-rich and nutrient-dense foods mentioned throughout this book. Depending on your hunger levels, your weight goal and how active you are, you might need to increase the number of calories you consume each day to maintain your weight and energy. We recommend that you continue to practice intermittent fasting in any way that suits you best, whether this means fasting a few hours daily or continuing to have a once-weekly cleanse day. To refresh your body, you might even choose to do three-day, liquid-only cleanses periodically throughout the year.

By paying attention to how you feel and customizing your diet accordingly, you can achieve and maintain your health for a lifetime. If you find yourself reverting to old habits that don't serve you, then consider simply restarting the three-day cleanse and repeating the 28-day meal plan. No matter what type of diet you decide to follow long-term, remember that including sources of collagen will provide benefits for your metabolism, joints, muscles and skin — both now and for years to come.

MY MULTI COLLAGEN PROTEIN EXPERIENCE

❚❚ I love this collagen; it has no taste and mixes well with my coffee. I feel so much better: my joints are less stiff and my skin looks better. I will be ordering more and will also try some other products. ❚❚

— Andrea H.

THE MULTI COLLAGEN MAKEOVER SHOPPING LIST

Here's a general overview of the foods you'll be consuming while following The Multi Collagen Makeover Plan:

FATS

- [ ] Avocado (about ½ per day)
- [ ] Oils (organic, high-quality) — coconut oil, avocado oil, extra virgin olive oil, chia seed oil, sesame oil
- [ ] Coconut cream (cream skimmed off of the top of canned coconut milk)
- [ ] Grass-fed butter
- [ ] Organic mayonnaise (made with avocado or olive oil)
- [ ] Ghee (clarified butter)
- [ ] Olives (about ¼ cup per day)

RED MEAT & POULTRY

(organic, grass-fed, pasture-raised):

- [ ] Beef*
- [ ] Bison
- [ ] Buffalo/elk
- [ ] Goat (chevon)
- [ ] Lamb
- [ ] Venison
- [ ] Chicken
- [ ] Turkey
- [ ] Duck
- [ ] Pheasant

SEAFOOD (wild-caught)

- [ ] Salmon
- [ ] Sardines
- [ ] Snapper
- [ ] Tilapia
- [ ] Tuna
- [ ] Bass
- [ ] Cod
- [ ] Halibut
- [ ] Haddock
- [ ] Ocean perch
- [ ] Orange roughy tuna
- [ ] Mahi mahi

EGGS

(pasture-raised, organic):

- [ ] Whole chicken or duck eggs (include yolk)

FERMENTED FOODS

- [ ] Fermented assorted veggies (parsnips, mushrooms, carrots, radishes, beets, etc.)
- [ ] Kimchi
- [ ] Raw apple cider vinegar
- [ ] Sauerkraut

*Note: If organic and grass-fed options aren't available, it's best to prioritize grass-fed red meat

VEGETABLES
(organic, if possible):

- [ ] Anise/fennel root
- [ ] Artichoke
- [ ] Arugula
- [ ] Asparagus
- [ ] Beet greens
- [ ] Bell peppers
- [ ] Bok choy
- [ ] Broccoli
- [ ] Cabbage
- [ ] Cauliflower
- [ ] Celery
- [ ] Chard
- [ ] Collard greens
- [ ] Cucumbers
- [ ] Dill pickles (no sugar added)
- [ ] Eggplant
- [ ] Garlic
- [ ] Green beans
- [ ] Kale
- [ ] Kohlrabi
- [ ] Leeks
- [ ] Lettuce (all types)
- [ ] Mushrooms (all types)
- [ ] Okra
- [ ] Olives
- [ ] Onions/shallots
- [ ] Potatoes (sweet, purple or red)
- [ ] Radishes
- [ ] Rhubarb
- [ ] Snow/sugar snap peas
- [ ] Spinach
- [ ] Sprouts
- [ ] Squash (spaghetti, summer, winter, acorn and butternut)
- [ ] Tomatoes
- [ ] Turnip
- [ ] Zucchini

DAIRY
(organic, grass-fed, raw, if possible):

- [ ] Hard cheeses (cheddar, jack, colby, parmesan, goat, manchego)
- [ ] Yogurt (full-fat, goat or A2 cow's milk)
- [ ] Kefir
- [ ] Cottage cheese
- [ ] Cream

BEVERAGES

- [ ] Coconut and almond milk (no added sugar)
- [ ] Coffee (preferably organic)
- [ ] Purified water
- [ ] Herbal infusions
- [ ] Water with sliced fruit, lemon or lime juice
- [ ] Fresh/raw juices
- [ ] Sparkling mineral water
- [ ] Tea (herbal, unsweetened, green, black, oolong, eleotin and yerba mate)

FRUITS
(organic, if possible):

- ☐ Acai berries
- ☐ Avocados
- ☐ Blackberries
- ☐ Blueberries
- ☐ Raspberries
- ☐ Strawberries
- ☐ Grapefruit
- ☐ Oranges
- ☐ Melon
- ☐ Apples
- ☐ Pears
- ☐ Peaches
- ☐ Plums
- ☐ Lemon
- ☐ Lime

NUTS & SEEDS

- ☐ Almonds
- ☐ Almond butter
- ☐ Brazil nuts
- ☐ Cashews
- ☐ Chia seeds
- ☐ Coconut butter
- ☐ Coconut flakes
- ☐ Flax seeds/flax meal
- ☐ Hazelnuts
- ☐ Hemp seeds
- ☐ Macadamia nuts

- ☐ Pecans
- ☐ Pine nuts
- ☐ Pistachios
- ☐ Pumpkin seeds/pepitas
- ☐ Sesame seeds
- ☐ Sunflower seeds
- ☐ Walnuts

LEGUMES
(we recommended soaking before cooking):

- ☐ Black beans
- ☐ Kidney beans
- ☐ Chickpeas/garbanzo beans
- ☐ Mung beans
- ☐ Adzuki beans
- ☐ Navy beans
- ☐ Lentils
- ☐ Red kidney beans
- ☐ Black-eyed peas
- ☐ Cannellini beans
- ☐ Butter beans
- ☐ Green peas

SWEETENERS

- ☐ Blackstrap molasses
- ☐ Monk fruit extract
- ☐ Pure maple syrup
- ☐ Raw honey
- ☐ Stevia

WHOLE/ANCIENT GRAINS

(we recommend soaking before cooking):

- [ ] Quinoa
- [ ] Brown rice
- [ ] Black rice
- [ ] Buckwheat
- [ ] Teff
- [ ] Amaranth
- [ ] Millet
- [ ] Oats

SEASONINGS & HERBS

- [ ] Apple cider vinegar
- [ ] Balsamic vinegar (with no sugar added and in moderation)
- [ ] Basil
- [ ] Bay leaves
- [ ] Black pepper
- [ ] Burdock root
- [ ] Cayenne
- [ ] Chamomile
- [ ] Cilantro
- [ ] Cinnamon (or cinnamon bark)
- [ ] Cocoa (raw)
- [ ] Coconut aminos
- [ ] Coconut vinegar
- [ ] Coriander
- [ ] Echinacea
- [ ] Garlic powder

- [ ] Ginger
- [ ] Himalayan pink salt
- [ ] Horseradish
- [ ] Hot peppers
- [ ] Lavender
- [ ] Licorice root
- [ ] Mint
- [ ] Mustard powder
- [ ] Oregano
- [ ] Parsley
- [ ] Peppercorn
- [ ] Peppermint
- [ ] Rosemary
- [ ] Sage
- [ ] Sea salt
- [ ] Tamari
- [ ] Thyme
- [ ] Turmeric

RECOMMENDED COLLAGEN SUPPLEMENTS

- [ ] Multi Collagen Protein
- [ ] Bone Broth Protein
- [ ] Bone Broth Collagen (optional)
- [ ] KetoCOLLAGEN (optional)

CHAPTER 7

RECIPES

BREAKFASTS AND BEVERAGES

Collagen Coffee

Golden Tea

Blueberry Bliss Collagen Smoothie

Carrot Ginger Bone Broth Shake

Cherry Vanilla Collagen Smoothie

Green Brain-Boosting Smoothie

Green Protein Smoothie

Mint Chocolate Smoothie

Peach Probiotic Smoothie

Pumpkin Pie Smoothie

Strawberry Coconut Bone Broth Smoothie

Turmeric Smoothie

MAIN DISHES

Beef and Butternut Squash Soup

Butternut Bisque

Creamy Tomato Soup

Indian Curry Soup

Meatball Soup

"Noodle" Bowls

Roasted Chicken with Roma
  Tomatoes and Onions

Spaghetti Squash with Roasted
  Chicken, Lemon and Parsley

Quinoa-Stuffed Bell Peppers

Chicken Tenders

Roasted Salmon with Kefir, Garlic
  and Avocado Sauce

SIDES

Ghee-Baked Brussels Sprouts

Grilled Asparagus

Maple Glazed Rosemary Carrots

Mashed Caul-tatoes

Strawberry Spinach Salad with
  Poppy Seed Dressing

Sweet Potato Fries

SNACKS

Blueberry Muffins

Blueberry Macadamia Bar

No-Bake Bone Broth Protein Bar

Cauliflower Hummus

Goat Cheese and Artichoke Dip

Kale Chips

DESSERTS

AB&J Milkshake

Banana Chia Pudding

Avocado Chocolate Mousse

Carrot Cake Squares

No-Bake Cashew Truffles

No-Bake Chocolate Chip Cookies

NOTE: *In all recipes, KetoCOLLAGEN may be substituted for Multi Collagen Protein and Bone Broth Collagen may be substituted for Bone Broth Protein as desired.*

BREAKFASTS AND BEVERAGES

COLLAGEN COFFEE

SERVES 1-2   **TOTAL TIME** 5 MINUTES

INGREDIENTS

1½ cup organic brewed coffee

1 tablespoon grass-fed butter

1 tablespoon coconut oil

1 scoop Multi Collagen Protein

DIRECTIONS

1. Brew the coffee to desired strength.

2. In a high-powered blender, place all ingredients and blend until well-combined.

GOLDEN TEA

SERVES 2   **TOTAL TIME** 5 M

INGREDIENTS

12 ounces unsweetened almond milk

½ cup water

1 scoop Bone Broth Protein Turmeric

1 tablespoon ghee

1 tablespoon raw honey

Cinnamon or pumpkin spice, to taste

DIRECTIONS

1. In a small saucepan over medium-low heat, combine the almond milk, water and bone broth powder. Warm for 2 minutes.

2. Add in the ghee and honey, and stir for another 2 minutes.

3. Stir again and pour into glasses. Top with the cinnamon or pumpkin spice.

**BLUEBERRY BLISS
COLLAGEN SMOOTHIE**

BLUEBERRY BLISS COLLAGEN SMOOTHIE

SERVES 1-2   **TOTAL TIME** 5 MINUTES

INGREDIENTS

1½ cups fresh or frozen blueberries

5 macadamia nuts

1 teaspoon vanilla extract

1 tablespoon raw honey or 2-3
   drops liquid stevia (optional)

2 tablespoons Multi Collagen Protein

2 cups full-fat, canned coconut milk

DIRECTIONS

1. In a high-powered blender,
    place all ingredients and blend
    until smooth, adding more
    coconut milk as needed.

CARROT GINGER BONE BROTH SHAKE

SERVES 1-2   **TOTAL TIME** 5 MINUTES

INGREDIENTS

3 cups grated carrots

1-inch piece fresh ginger, peeled
   and chopped

3 tablespoons Bone Broth Protein Pure

1¼ cups full-fat, canned coconut milk

1 tablespoon raw honey

Handful of ice cubes

DIRECTIONS

1. In a high-powered blender,
    place all ingredients and
    blend until smooth. Serve
    immediately.

CHERRY VANILLA COLLAGEN SMOOTHIE

SERVES 1   **TOTAL TIME** 5 MINUTES

INGREDIENTS

1 cup unsweetened almond milk

1 cup frozen cherries

1 scoop Bone Broth Protein Vanilla

3-4 ice cubes

DIRECTIONS

1. In a high-powered blender, place all ingredients and blend until smooth, adding more almond milk as needed.

GREEN BRAIN-BOOSTING SMOOTHIE

SERVES 1-2   **TOTAL TIME** 5 MINUTES

INGREDIENTS

½ avocado

½ banana

½ cup blueberries

1 scoop Bone Broth Protein Vanilla

6 walnuts

½ cup water

DIRECTIONS

1. In a high-powered blender, place all ingredients and blend until smooth.

GREEN
BRAIN-BOOSTING
SMOOTHIE

GREEN PROTEIN SMOOTHIE

SERVES 1-2   **TOTAL TIME** 5 MINUTES

INGREDIENTS

½ cup unsweetened almond milk

½ cucumber

½ avocado

1 cup spinach

1 teaspoon matcha

2 celery stalks

1 tablespoon chia seeds

1 scoop Bone Broth Protein Vanilla

DIRECTIONS

1. In a high-powered blender, place all ingredients and blend until smooth.

MINT CHOCOLATE SMOOTHIE

SERVES 1-2   **TOTAL TIME** 5 M

INGREDIENTS

1½ cups unsweetened almond milk

1-2 drops peppermint extract

2 tablespoons cocoa powder

1 scoop Bone Broth Protein Chocolate

6 ice cubes

Cacao nibs, to taste

DIRECTIONS

1. In a high-powered blender, place all ingredients, except the cacao nibs, and blend until smooth. Add more almond milk or ice as needed.

2. Top with the cacao nibs.

PEACH PROBIOTIC SMOOTHIE

SERVES 1-2   **TOTAL TIME** 5 MINUTES

INGREDIENTS

½ banana

¾ cup frozen peaches

½ cup full-fat, canned coconut milk
  or goat milk kefir (or yogurt)

1½ cups unsweetened almond milk

½ teaspoon ground cinnamon

1 scoop Bone Broth Protein Vanilla

⅛ teaspoon vanilla extract

DIRECTIONS

1. In a high-powered blender, place all ingredients and blend until smooth.

PUMPKIN PIE SMOOTHIE

SERVES 1-2   **TOTAL TIME** 5 MINUTES

INGREDIENTS

½ cup pumpkin purée

½ cup cooked butternut squash

½ teaspoon pumpkin pie spice

1½ cups almond milk

1 scoop Bone Broth Protein Vanilla

DIRECTIONS

1. In a high-powered blender, place all ingredients and blend until smooth, adding more almond milk as needed.

PEACH PROBIOTIC
SMOOTHIE

STRAWBERRY COCONUT BONE BROTH SMOOTHIE

SERVES 4   **TOTAL TIME** 5 MINUTES

INGREDIENTS

¾ cup full-fat, canned coconut milk

1 tablespoon Bone Broth Protein
   Vanilla

3 cups strawberries

1 cup ice

DIRECTIONS

1. In a high-powered blender, place all ingredients and blend until smooth, adding more coconut milk as needed.

TURMERIC SMOOTHIE

SERVES 1-2   **TOTAL TIME** 5 MINUTES

INGREDIENTS

½ cup unsweetened almond milk

1 teaspoon ground ginger

1 teaspoon cinnamon

½ teaspoon Himalayan pink salt

1 teaspoon vanilla extract

1 tablespoon coconut oil

1 scoop Bone Broth Protein Turmeric

4-6 ice cubes

Stevia or monk fruit, to taste

DIRECTIONS

1. In a high-powered blender, place all ingredients and blend until smooth.

**STRAWBERRY COCONUT
BONE BROTH SMOOTHIE**

MAIN
DISHES

BEEF AND BUTTERNUT SQUASH SOUP

SERVES 6   **TOTAL TIME** 35 MINUTES

INGREDIENTS

**4 scoops Bone Broth Protein Pure mixed in
6 cups water (or 6 cups beef bone broth)**

1½ teaspoons ground ginger

1 teaspoon chipotle pepper

1 teaspoon cumin

½ teaspoon sea salt

1 pound beef, sliced or cubed

1 yellow onion, diced

1 medium butternut squash, cubed

DIRECTIONS

1. In a large pot over medium heat, bring the bone broth, spices and sea salt to a simmer.

2. Add the remaining ingredients and return to a simmer. Reduce the heat to low and simmer for 25 minutes.

3. Serve warm.

BUTTERNUT BISQUE

SERVES 4   **TOTAL TIME** 1 HOUR

INGREDIENTS

4 tablespoons ghee

1 red onion, minced

1 Granny Smith apple, peeled, cored and chopped

2 teaspoons dried sage

1 butternut squash, peeled, seeded and cut into chunks

3 scoops Bone Broth Protein Pure mixed with 4½ cups water (or 4½ cups beef bone broth)

1 teaspoon nutmeg

Sea salt and pepper, to taste

DIRECTIONS

1. In a large pot over medium heat, melt the ghee. Add the onion, apple and sage, stirring occasionally, for about 8 minutes.

2. Add the squash and bone broth. Bring to a simmer and cook for 15-20 minutes, or until the squash is fork tender.

3. Using an immersion blender, purée the squash until smooth. (Note: Use caution blending hot liquids.)

4. Heat through and season with the nutmeg, sea salt and pepper before serving.

CREAMY TOMATO SOUP

SERVES 6-8   **TOTAL TIME** 20 MINUTES

INGREDIENTS

3 cloves garlic, pressed or minced

1 tablespoon coconut oil

4 cups diced tomatoes

1¾ cups full-fat, canned coconut milk

½ teaspoon sea salt

2 teaspoons apple cider vinegar

4 cups beef bone broth

4 scoops Multi Collagen Protein

Fresh basil, minced, to taste

Fresh cracked pepper, to taste

DIRECTIONS

1. In a medium pot over medium-low heat, sauté the garlic in the coconut oil for 5 minutes, or until lightly browned.

2. In a high-powered blender, add the tomatoes, coconut milk, salt, vinegar, bone broth and collagen powder, blending until well-combined.

3. Pour the mixture into the pot, stirring occasionally, and bring the mixture to a simmer.

4. Simmer for 10-15 minutes and allow the soup to rest for 5 minutes before serving.

5. Serve topped with the fresh basil and pepper.

INDIAN CURRY SOUP

SERVES 4   **TOTAL TIME** 35 MINUTES

INGREDIENTS

4 scoops Bone Broth Protein Pure

   mixed in 6 cups water

1 tablespoon fresh grated ginger root

3 tablespoons curry powder

1 yellow onion, chopped

2 cups small cauliflower florets, chopped

2 red peppers, chopped

1 teaspoon cayenne pepper

1¾ cups full-fat, canned coconut milk

DIRECTIONS

1. In a large pot over medium heat, bring the bone broth and ginger to a simmer. Add in the collagen powder, curry powder, onion, cauliflower, red peppers and cayenne.

2. Bring to a boil, then reduce the heat to medium-low and simmer for 15 minutes.

3. Add in the coconut milk, stir until well-combined and cook for an additional 5-10 minutes.

4. Allow the soup to rest for 5 minutes, then serve and enjoy.

MEATBALL SOUP

SERVES 4-6   **TOTAL TIME** 50 MINUTES

INGREDIENTS

1½ pounds ground bison or beef

2 eggs, whisked

½ teaspoon + 1 teaspoon sea salt, divided

1 teaspoon smoked paprika or cayenne

2 tablespoons coconut oil

3 scoops Bone Broth Protein Pure

   mixed with 6 cups water

2 bay leaves

4 carrots, peeled and chopped

1 large sweet potato, chopped

1 cup green beans

1 cup green peas

2 tomatoes, chopped

DIRECTIONS

1. In a medium bowl, mix together the meat, eggs, ½ teaspoon salt and paprika or cayenne. Roll into small meatballs.

2. In a large pot over medium heat, heat the oil. Add the meatballs and cook for 5-8 minutes, or until brown.

3. Add the bone broth, remaining salt, bay leaves, carrots and sweet potato, bringing to a simmer over medium-high heat.

4. Add the remaining ingredients and simmer for 20 minutes, or until the sweet potato is tender. Serve immediately.

"NOODLE" BOWLS

SERVES 4   **TOTAL TIME** 50 MINUTES

INGREDIENTS

3 chicken breasts

2 tablespoons coconut oil,
  melted and divided

1 tablespoon sea salt

1 tablespoon black pepper

½ medium red onion, diced

3 stalks celery, chopped

6 carrots, chopped

4 cups chopped kale, stems
  removed

5 scoops Bone Broth Protein
  Pure mixed in 8 cups water

3 medium zucchini, spiralized
  into noodles

Fresh basil, to taste

DIRECTIONS

1. Preheat the oven to 325 degrees F.

2. Line a baking sheet with parchment paper
   and place the chicken on the sheet, drizzle
   with 1 tablespoon of the coconut oil and add
   the salt and pepper. Place in the oven and
   bake for 30 minutes.

3. In a large stockpot over medium heat, add
   the remaining coconut oil, onion, celery and
   carrots and cook for 8-10 minutes.

4. Add in the kale and bone broth. Stir
   to combine.

5. Reduce the heat to low and let simmer for
   25 minutes.

6. Take the chicken out of the oven and allow
   to cool for 5 minutes.

7. Using two forks, shred the chicken and add to
   the stockpot. Simmer for another 15 minutes.

8. Add in the spiralized zucchini, stirring to
   combine.

9. Add more sea salt and pepper to taste and
   serve topped with the fresh basil.

ROASTED CHICKEN WITH ROMA TOMATOES AND ONIONS

SERVES 4   **TOTAL TIME** 40 MINUTES

INGREDIENTS

2 teaspoons coconut oil

2 pounds chicken thighs, skin on and bone in

2 tablespoons ghee

2 tablespoons garlic, minced

½ teaspoon sea salt

½ teaspoon black pepper

½ white onion, sliced

1 cup Roma tomatoes, sliced

½ cup chicken bone broth

Fresh basil, to taste

DIRECTIONS

1. Preheat the oven to 425 degrees F.

2. In a skillet over medium-high heat, heat the coconut oil.

3. Pat the chicken thighs with a paper towel to remove excess moisture and set aside. In a bowl, mix together the ghee, garlic, salt and pepper and place the mixture under the skin of the chicken and on the outside.

4. Place the chicken thighs in the skillet skin down and sear for 5 minutes, or until browned.

5. Flip the chicken over and add the sliced onions and tomatoes.

6. Pour the bone broth around the chicken.

7. Place the skillet in the oven and roast the chicken for 15-20 minutes, or until the chicken reaches an internal temperature of 165 F.

8. Let cool for 5 minutes and top with the basil before serving.

SPAGHETTI SQUASH WITH ROASTED CHICKEN, LEMON AND PARSLEY

SERVES 4   **TOTAL TIME** 1 HOUR

INGREDIENTS

1 medium spaghetti squash

2 tablespoons ghee (divided)

1½ pounds chicken thighs, skin on and bone in

¼ teaspoon sea salt

¼ teaspoon black pepper

2 tablespoons chopped garlic

Juice of 1 lemon

½ cup chicken broth

1 scoop Multi Collagen Protein

¼ cup chopped parsley (divided)

DIRECTIONS

1. Preheat the oven to 425 degrees F. Cut the spaghetti squash in half and scoop out the seeds. Place the squash face down and cook for 40-50 minutes, or until the squash is soft.

2. Set aside and let cool, and then use a fork to scrape the spaghetti out.

3. In a large skillet over medium-high heat, heat 1 tablespoon of the ghee and sprinkle the outside of the chicken with the salt and pepper.

4. Add the chicken to the pan skin side down, sear for 5 minutes and then remove the chicken and set on a plate.

5. Add the garlic to the skillet and brown for about 30 seconds. Then add the lemon juice, broth, collagen powder and 1 tablespoon of the parsley and stir.

6. Add the chicken back to the pan, skin side up, and roast in the oven for 10-12 minutes, or until the chicken's internal temperature reaches 165 degrees F.

7. Toss some of the hot spaghetti squash with the remaining ghee. Divide the spaghetti squash onto four plates and top with the chicken and more parsley and serve.

QUINOA-STUFFED BELL PEPPERS

SERVES 2-4   **TOTAL TIME** 45 MINUTES

INGREDIENTS

6 cups water

2 cups quinoa, rinsed and drained

2 scoops Bone Broth Protein Pure

2 bell peppers, halved and seeded

Sea salt and pepper, to taste

1 teaspoon coconut oil

1 onion, diced

1 zucchini, chopped

2 tablespoons minced garlic

1 tablespoon dried Italian seasoning

½ cup fresh parsley, chopped

1 cup crumbled goat cheese

DIRECTIONS

1. Preheat the oven to 450 degrees F.

2. In a medium pot, add the water, quinoa and protein powder. Cook according to package directions.

3. Meanwhile, sprinkle the bell peppers with the salt and pepper. Place the peppers on a baking sheet and roast cut side down for 20 minutes, or until the skin begins to char. Remove from the oven and reduce the oven temperature to 375 degrees F.

4. While the bell peppers roast, in a skillet over medium heat, melt the oil. Add the onion, zucchini, garlic and Italian seasoning. Season with more salt and pepper. Cook, stirring occasionally, for 10-12 minutes, or until the vegetables are tender. Add the quinoa to the skillet. Sprinkle with the parsley and stir to combine.

5. Turn the bell peppers cut side up and fill the halves evenly with the quinoa mixture. Heat in the oven until warmed through. Served topped with the cheese.

CHICKEN TENDERS

SERVES 4   **TOTAL TIME** 20 MINUTES

INGREDIENTS

4 chicken breasts, sliced into strips

2 eggs

1 scoop Multi Collagen Protein

Italian seasoning, to taste

sea salt, to taste

1 cup brown rice or coconut flour

1 tablespoon coconut oil

DIRECTIONS

1. In a medium bowl, beat the eggs slightly. Add the collagen powder, Italian seasoning and salt, mixing well.

2. Dip the strips of chicken in the egg mixture, and then coat with the flour.

3. In a medium frying pan over medium heat, melt the coconut oil. Fry the chicken, turning once, until golden brown and cooked through. Serve warm.

ROASTED SALMON WITH KEFIR, GARLIC AND AVOCADO SAUCE

SERVES 4   **TOTAL TIME** 45 MINUTES

INGREDIENTS

Fish:

1½ pounds wild-caught salmon fillet, skin on, pin bones removed

2 tablespoons olive oil

½ teaspoon sea salt

½-1 teaspoon black pepper

2 tablespoons lemon juice

Sauce:

1 avocado, peeled and pitted

2 cups kefir

2 scoops Multi Collagen Protein

2 cloves garlic, peeled and smashed

¼-½ teaspoon sea salt

DIRECTIONS

1. Preheat the oven to 425 degrees F.

2. Place the salmon on a baking sheet lined with parchment paper, rub with the olive oil and coat evenly with the salt and pepper. Drizzle on the lemon juice. Cook for 15 minutes, or until it flakes when gently pressed.

3. Meanwhile, in a high-powered blender, add the avocado, kefir, collagen powder, garlic and salt and blend on high until well-combined. Add more kefir as needed.

4. Remove the salmon from the oven. Peel the skin off and break the flesh into chunks. Plate and drizzle with the sauce. Serve immediately.

SIDES

GHEE-BAKED BRUSSELS SPROUTS

SERVES 1-2   **TOTAL TIME** 35 MINUTES

INGREDIENTS

1 bunch Brussels sprouts, halved

1 small red onion, cut into crescents

½ cup walnuts, chopped

**2 tablespoons ghee or coconut
   oil, melted**

Sea salt and black pepper, to taste

DIRECTIONS

1. Preheat the oven to 425 degrees F.

2. In a medium bowl, combine the Brussels sprouts, onion and walnuts. Mix in the ghee until evenly distributed.

3. Sprinkle with the salt and pepper, and then spread the mixture out onto a rimmed baking sheet.

4. Roast for 35 to 40 minutes, or until slightly browned.

GRILLED ASPARAGUS

SERVES 2-3   **TOTAL TIME** 15 MINUTES

INGREDIENTS

3 tablespoons coconut oil

1 bunch asparagus

¼ cup parsley, chopped

5 cloves garlic, chopped

DIRECTIONS

1. In a skillet over medium-high heat, melt the coconut oil.

2. Add the remaining ingredients to the pan. Cover and cook for 10 minutes, stirring occasionally. Continue to cook until desired tenderness is achieved.

MAPLE GLAZED ROSEMARY CARROTS

SERVES 4-6   **TOTAL TIME** 25 MINUTES

INGREDIENTS

3 cups carrots, peeled and sliced

2 tablespoons coconut oil

2 tablespoons maple syrup

1 ½ tablespoons chopped
  fresh rosemary

½ teaspoon sea salt

½ teaspoon black pepper

DIRECTIONS

1. In a skillet over medium heat, cook the carrots in just enough water to cover them. Bring to a boil and simmer until the water has evaporated and the carrots are soft.

2. Stir in the remaining ingredients and cook for another 5-10 minutes over low heat.

3. Serve immediately.

MASHED CAUL-TATOES

SERVES 4   **TOTAL TIME** 25 MINUTES

INGREDIENTS

1 medium head cauliflower

2 scoops Multi Collagen Protein

4 tablespoons ghee

½ teaspoon sea salt

½ teaspoon black pepper

Pinch of parsley

DIRECTIONS

1. Steam the cauliflower for 10 minutes, or until the florets are tender.

2. In a food processor, add the cauliflower, collagen powder, ghee, salt and pepper. Process until smooth.

3. Serve immediately, topping with the parsley.

MAPLE GLAZED
ROSEMARY
CARROTS
▼

135

STRAWBERRY SPINACH SALAD WITH POPPY SEED DRESSING

SERVES 4-6   **TOTAL TIME** 12 MINUTES

INGREDIENTS

Dressing:

½ cup extra virgin olive oil

2 tablespoons apple cider vinegar

1½ tablespoons poppy seeds

1 tablespoon lemon juice

Salt and pepper, to taste

Salad:

6 cups spinach

2 cups strawberries, chopped

½ red onion, diced

1 avocado, diced

¼-½ cup goat feta cheese

¼ cup sprouted almonds, chopped

DIRECTIONS

1. In a small bowl, mix all the dressing ingredients until well-combined. Set aside.

2. In a large bowl, combine all the salad ingredients.

3. Pour the dressing onto the salad and mix until well-combined.

4. Refrigerate for 20 minutes and serve.

SWEET POTATO FRIES

SERVES 3-6   **TOTAL TIME** 1 HOUR

INGREDIENTS

1-1½ pounds sweet potatoes

¼ cup coconut oil, melted

½ teaspoon sea salt

½ teaspoon paprika

¼ teaspoon cinnamon

DIRECTIONS

1. Preheat the oven to 425 degrees F. Peel the potatoes and cut into ½-inch wide strips.

2. Place all ingredients in a sealable plastic bag and shake until the potatoes are completely coated. Spread onto a baking sheet.

3. Cook for 30-45 minutes, turning every 10 minutes.

4. Transfer immediately to a paper towel-lined plate and serve warm.

SNACKS

BLUEBERRY MUFFINS

SERVES 12   **TOTAL TIME** 40 MINUTES

INGREDIENTS

1 cup gluten-free oat flour

½ cup almond flour

½ teaspoon baking powder

¼ teaspoon sea salt

6 scoops Multi Collagen Protein

3 eggs

½ cup raw honey

½ cup applesauce

1 teaspoon vanilla extract

1 teaspoon apple cider vinegar

⅛ cup coconut oil, melted,
   plus more for greasing pan

1 cup fresh or frozen blueberries

DIRECTIONS

1. Preheat the oven to 350 degrees F.

2. Grease a standard muffin tin with coconut oil and set aside.

3. In a large mixing bowl, whisk together the oat flour, almond flour, baking powder, salt and collagen powder.

4. In a separate bowl, combine the eggs, honey, applesauce, vanilla, apple cider vinegar and melted coconut oil. Stir until well-combined.

5. Slowly add the dry mixture into the wet mixture and stir well.

6. Fold the blueberries into the batter.

7. Bake for 30 minutes, or until golden brown on top.

BLUEBERRY MACADAMIA BAR

SERVES 6   **TOTAL TIME** 2 HOURS, 15 MINUTES

INGREDIENTS

½ cup melted coconut butter

¼ cup raw honey

1 teaspoon vanilla extract

⅛ teaspoon sea salt

4 scoops Bone Broth Protein Vanilla

½ cup dried blueberries

½ cup chopped raw macadamia nuts

3 tablespoons water

DIRECTIONS

1. In a medium bowl, whisk together the butter, honey, vanilla and salt. Add the bone broth powder and combine. Add the remaining ingredients and combine again.

2. Pour into a greased loaf pan. Refrigerate for 1-2 hours, and then cut into bar or cookie shapes.

NO-BAKE BONE BROTH PROTEIN BAR

SERVES 12   **TOTAL TIME** 1 HOUR, 10 MINUTES

INGREDIENTS

4 cups cashews

3 cups Medjool dates, pitted

2 tablespoons cashew butter

2 teaspoons vanilla extract

2 teaspoons cinnamon

4 tablespoons Bone Broth
   Protein Vanilla

2 tablespoons water

⅛ teaspoon sea salt

DIRECTIONS

1. In a food processor, pulse the cashews until small chunks form. Add in the remaining ingredients and process on high until the dough forms, scraping the sides as needed.

2. In a cupcake pan filled with liners, evenly distribute the mixture.

3. Cover and freeze for 1 hour before serving.

CAULIFLOWER HUMMUS

SERVES 4   **TOTAL TIME** 1 HOUR

INGREDIENTS

1 medium-sized cauliflower

½ cup tahini

3-4 scoops Multi Collagen Protein

2 tablespoons olive oil

2 large garlic cloves

⅓ cup lemon juice

1 teaspoon sea salt

½ teaspoon black pepper

¼ cup chopped parsley (optional)

1 tablespoon olive oil (optional)

DIRECTIONS

1. Preheat the oven to 425 degrees F, and line a baking sheet with parchment paper.

2. Remove the florets from the cauliflower and place them onto the baking sheet. Toss in a small amount of olive oil and roast for 15 minutes.

3. In a food processor, add the roasted cauliflower, tahini, collagen powder, olive oil, garlic, lemon juice, salt and pepper and process until smooth.

4. Pour the hummus into an airtight container and place in the refrigerator until cold.

5. Serve in a bowl and top with the parsley and olive oil (if desired).

GOAT CHEESE AND ARTICHOKE DIP

SERVES 2-4   **TOTAL TIME** 5 MINUTES

INGREDIENTS

1 can artichoke hearts, drained

1 pound chèvre goat cheese

1 scoop Multi Collagen Protein

2 tablespoons olive oil

2 teaspoons lemon juice

1 garlic clove, minced

1 tablespoon parsley

1 tablespoon chives

½ tablespoon basil

Sea salt and black pepper, to taste

Dash of cayenne pepper

½ cup Pecorino, grated

DIRECTIONS

1. In a food processor, add all ingredients, except the Pecorino, and process until well-combined and creamy.

2. Top with the freshly grated pecorino and serve.

KALE CHIPS

SERVES 2-4   **TOTAL TIME** 15 MINUTES

INGREDIENTS

1 bunch kale

2 tablespoons grapeseed oil

1 tablespoon lemon juice

¼ teaspoon sea salt

DIRECTIONS

1. Preheat the oven to 350 degrees F.

2. Chop the kale into ½-inch pieces.

3. In a large bowl, place all ingredients and massage the oil, lemon juice and sea salt into the kale using your hands.

4. Place the kale on a parchment-lined baking sheets and bake for 12 minutes.

5. Remove from the oven and serve.

DESSERTS

AB&J MILKSHAKE

SERVES 1-2   **TOTAL TIME** 5 MINUTES

INGREDIENTS

½ avocado

3 tablespoons almond butter

1 cup unsweetened almond milk

4-6 ice cubes

½ cup strawberries

Juice of ½ lime

1 scoop Bone Broth Protein Vanilla

DIRECTIONS

1. In a high-powered blender, place all ingredients and blend until smooth.

BANANA CHIA PUDDING

SERVES 3-4   **TOTAL TIME** 30 MINUTES

INGREDIENTS

1 cup full-fat, canned coconut milk

¼ cup ground chia seeds

5 tablespoons raw honey

1 banana

1 scoop Bone Broth Protein Vanilla

¼ teaspoon pumpkin spice or cinnamon

DIRECTIONS

1. In a food processor or blender, place all ingredients and process/blend for 1 minute.

2. Refrigerate for 10-15 minutes before serving.

AVOCADO CHOCOLATE MOUSSE

SERVES 6-8   **TOTAL TIME** 5-10 MINUTES

INGREDIENTS

1 teaspoon vanilla extract

1½ cups mashed avocado
  (about 2-3 avocados)

2 scoops Bone Broth
  Protein Chocolate

¼ cup cacao powder

½ cup water
  (optional for texture)

DIRECTIONS

1. In a food processor, add the vanilla, avocado, protein powder and cacao. Process until creamy, stopping to scrape down the sides of the bowl with a spatula if needed.

2. Add the water, if desired, and process until smooth.

3. Serve at room temperature or chilled. Store in a sealed container in the refrigerator up to three days or in the freezer up to two weeks.

CARROT CAKE SQUARES

SERVES 10   **TOTAL TIME** 35 MINUTES

INGREDIENTS

1 cup dates, halved and pitted

½ cup melted coconut oil

1 teaspoon vanilla extract

2 teaspoons cinnamon

2 eggs

¼ teaspoon sea salt

¾ cup Bone Broth Protein Vanilla

1½ cups shredded carrots

½ cup walnut pieces

1½ cups oats

¾ cups raisins

DIRECTIONS

1. Preheat the oven to 375 degrees F.

2. Line an 8 x 8-inch baking dish with parchment paper.

3. In a food processor, add the dates, coconut oil, vanilla and cinnamon. Process until well-combined.

4. In a medium mixing bowl, whisk together the eggs, salt and protein powder until well-combined.

5. Add the date mixture into the egg mixture and whisk until incorporated.

6. Add the remaining ingredients and mix well.

7. Bake for 20-25 minutes, or until golden brown on outside.

NO-BAKE CASHEW TRUFFLES

SERVES 6-8   **TOTAL TIME** 10 MINUTES

INGREDIENTS

1 cup cashews

2 tablespoons cashew butter

6 Medjool dates, pitted

½ teaspoon cinnamon

1 teaspoon vanilla extract

3 tablespoons coconut oil, melted and cooled

1 tablespoon full-fat, canned coconut milk

3-4 scoops Bone Broth Protein Chocolate

1 teaspoon cinnamon

DIRECTIONS

1. In a food processor, process the cashews until small chunks form. Add the cashew butter, dates, cinnamon, vanilla, coconut oil, coconut milk and bone broth powder, blending until the mixture becomes pasty.

2. Using your hands, roll the dough into bite-sized balls.

3. Dust with the cinnamon and place in the refrigerator for 1 hour, or until firm.

NO-BAKE CHOCOLATE CHIP COOKIES

SERVES 6 **TOTAL TIME** 2 HOURS, 10 MINUTES

INGREDIENTS

1 ½ cups raw almond butter

¼ cup raw honey

1 teaspoon vanilla extract

¼ teaspoon sea salt

1 scoop Bone Broth Protein Pure

½ cup dark chocolate chips

DIRECTIONS

1. In a medium bowl, stir together the almond butter, honey, vanilla and salt. Add the bone broth powder and combine thoroughly.

2. Stir in the chocolate chips and place in the refrigerator for about 2 hours.

3. Remove from the refrigerator, form into cookie shapes and enjoy.